Jackson's Chameleon

Jackson's Chameleons as Pets

Jackson's Chameleon book for care, feeding, handling, health and common myths.

by

Jonathan Durham

Table of Contents

Introduction

The word Chameleon comes from the Greek words "Chamai" and "Leon" meaning 'Earth Lion.'

These creatures originate from the lizard family and in their natural habitat tend to live in trees, although some species can also be found in low shrubs and scrubs.

Chameleons are unusual because they can change the colour of their skin; a fact most people know even if they've never seen one in real life. This, along with their beautiful colours and patterns and interesting behaviour, have made chameleons more popular in recent years and they are now some of the most sought after reptiles.

This book focuses on the Jackson's Chameleon.

Chapter 1: The Jackson's Chameleon

Introduction

The Jackson's Chameleon originates from Kenya and Tanzania in East Africa. These creatures were named after the famous English naturalist Sir Frederick John Jackson who carried out extensive expeditions to Kenya where he collected several species of birds and reptiles. As Jackson's Chameleons are found in the land of the Kikuyu (an ethnic group in Kenya) they are also known as the Kikuyu Three Horned Chameleons.

In the early 1970s a pet shop owner on the island of Oahu obtained a permit to import Jackson's Chameleons from Kenya with the hope of selling them. When they arrived he discovered they were thin, dehydrated and generally unhealthy. Thinking they would regain their strength quicker outdoors he released them onto a tree in his back garden, planning to collect them all later. Of course, these animals ventured out of the yard and into the wild where they mated and became an invasive species, which can now be found all over the island.

Their natural habitats are cool, humid mountain slopes or rainforests where there is significant rainfall and vegetation as well as dense foliage to hide in.

Jackson's Chameleons are arboreal creatures and, like most other chameleons, will rarely venture down onto the floor as their feet and body shape – perfectly designed for life in trees – prevent fast movement, making them more susceptible to predators.

There are three recognised subspecies of the Jackson's Chameleons. These are:

The Jackson's Chameleon – not the largest or the smallest they are recognisable as their horns have a darker hue than the other subspecies.

The Dwarf Jackson's Chameleon which, as you've probably guessed by the name, are the smallest of the sub-species and are identifiable by a lighter coloured crest.

Yellow Crested Jackson's Chameleon, the largest of the subspecies, are identifiable by the yellow colouring around their heads.

The latter two are most commonly found in captivity although many people just refer to them as Jackson's Chameleons without identifying which species they are and the care is pretty much the same for all.

Although they are a popular type of chameleon to keep in captivity, they are less hardy than some other species of chameleons such as the Veiled Chameleon or the Panther Chameleon and therefore are not recommended for novice chameleon owners and should definitely not be kept by anybody who has never owned a reptile before.

Size
Depending on the sub-species, a male can range from 22-25.5 centimetres (9-15 inches) in total length, including the tail. Females tend to be smaller at around 17-25 centimetres (7-10 inches) from snout to tail.

Although smaller than some other breeds of chameleons, you will still need a fairly large cage so before buying assess whether you have room for it. The upshot of owning any type of chameleon is that they like to climb, therefore your cage needs to be vertical rather than horizontal. Unlike a fish tank that tends to take up a whole wall, your chameleon cage will need to be tall, taking space that would not necessarily be used otherwise.

Life Span

In captivity a healthy male Jackson's Chameleon can be expected to live approximately 5-10 years. Of course this longevity is dependent upon its habitat being suitable enough to meet all of its needs. Some owners report that their chameleons have made it to the ten year mark or more whereas others only have them for six months to a year. You need to research thoroughly before you even *think* about purchasing one as they are incredibly sensitive creatures which have very specific care requirements.

A female Jackson's Chameleon, no matter how well it's cared for and how perfect its environment is, will typically have a life span of only 3-5 years. A female's role is to reproduce and once they have been mated it can take a toll on their bodies, which results in a shorter life than their male counterparts. As Jackson's Chameleons give birth to live babies they will not produce infertile clutches of eggs like some other breeds of chameleons so you could, theoretically, extend the life of your female Jackson's Chameleon by not breeding her however if you want a single chameleon as a pet then a male would always be recommended simply because of the longer life spans.

Jackson's Chameleons can develop a lot of medical problems but if you learn how to properly look after these unique creatures and know what symptoms to watch out for then there's no reason why you can't raise them successfully and give them a fairly long and happy life.

A lot of owners report that they notice their chameleons getting more delicate and tend to lose their energy around the five year mark. Just like us humans, the older they get the more susceptible they are to illness and injury.

Interesting Features

If you ask an owner why they find chameleons so interesting their reply will be the amazing adaptions they have, many of which are unusual in a pet.

Horns

The Jackson's Chameleon is identifiable by the three horns on their faces, one which extends from the nose, known as the rostral horn and two above each superior orbital ridge above their eyes, known as the pre-ocular horns. This feature gives them a look of a miniature rhinoceros or triceratops.

It is thought that a chameleon's horns are for display and combat. Scientists have witnessed Jackson's Chameleons charging towards each other with open mouths, their heads lowered in order to ram their opponent with their horns. Those males with longer horns tend to have an advantage because they can strike their enemy first. Whilst this display may simply be a warning, an accidental poke from the pre-orbital or the rostral horn in an eye or a lung can cause enormous damage and is a reason why you should keep your chameleons separate.

Only the males tend to have these horns although the females of some sub-species can sometimes have less developed ones.

An interesting fact is that these horns grow throughout their whole lives.

Eyes

A chameleon's eyes are globe shaped and protrude from their head. For a reptile, the chameleon has great eyesight and can see small insects from fairly long distances but what makes them particularly special is that they can swivel their eyes independently from each other, meaning the chameleon can look both behind and in front at the same time. When searching for food a chameleon will often move both eyes in different directions until it finds a target. Once this has been spotted the clever creature will usually focus both eyes on the prey in order to judge the distance and its aim. Another advantage of these amazing eyes is that the chameleon can keep one eye on its prey whilst it creeps towards it yet also be on the lookout for predators.

Projectile Tongue

This is one of the chameleon's most remarkable adaptations. Approximately one and a half times the length of its body, the tongue is hollow with a large sticky tip. Scientists have discovered that the tongue works a bit like a catapult. When the chameleon sees its, prey a contracting muscle will shoot its tongue out at lightning speed. The prey will get trapped on the sticky pad and then crushed to prevent escape. A different muscle then draws the tongue back up into the mouth where it's bunched up like an accordion until it's needed again.

To see this in action place food at different distances and watch the chameleon snap it up. It takes around 0.07 seconds and they have around a ninety percent success rate- so if you blink you'll miss it!

Legs And Feet

These are unique because their toes are fused together, giving them a pincer look. Each foot has three toes opposing two toes, which work in a similar way that our opposing thumb and other fingers do. On the front they have the three toes on the inside and the two on the outside whereas the back feet are the opposite. The sharp claws on the end and the small, rough scales beneath enable the chameleon to grip onto twigs, making them expert climbers.

Gait

This is slow and deliberate and is thought to be part of the chameleon's strategy of escaping unnoticed and aiding it to camouflage itself. Sometimes you may see them rocking back and forth as they move, giving the effect of a leaf moving in the breeze, this illusion is aided by the creatures flattened sides, enabling it to hide in the tree branches. If necessary, chameleons are capable of running quickly for short distances but they shouldn't need to do this very often in captivity.

Tail

This is prehensile, meaning it has evolved to grasp and acts almost as a fifth foot by twisting and twining itself around branches, enabling the chameleon to secure itself in the trees. Although the Jackson's Chameleon has a fantastic grip with its adapted feet, it can use its long tail as a safety net when needed in case it loses its footing. Often in the wild, the chameleon will use its tail when hunting as it can allow them to extend a centimetre closer to their prey, which although it doesn't sound a lot, combined with their long tongue, can make a huge difference. Their tails are so powerful the chameleon can use it to pull its entire body back up onto a branch.

Colour

Young Jackson's Chameleons tend to be brownish in colour which changes to a brighter green at around four to five months of age. Their lips and the base of their eyes, as well as their claws, tend to be yellow whilst the interior of their mouths are pink.

Like other chameleon species they can change colour at certain times and this is caused by special cells. Although this is probably the chameleon's most famous characteristic, it is also misunderstood. Who hasn't seen a cartoon or a TV programme depicting a chameleon changing colour so dramatically on any background, plain or patterned, that all you can see are its eyes? Sorry to disappoint you but placing your new pet on tartan material won't cause it to appear checked nor is it solely for camouflage. In fact the ability to mimic its background colour is limited to lighter or darker coloration and it is affected more by temperature or mood.

When the chameleon is cold it will usually darken as this attracts the heat, when it is warm it will turn a lighter shade in order to reflect the heat away from its body.

Colour changes are also used to communicate, showing whether the animal is angry or scared or used in territorial displays to depict who is the more dominant. With two males confronting one another these changes can be dramatic – becoming suddenly brighter and colour patterns that were previously hidden or insignificant may appear as vivid stripes, blotches and spots. The brighter the colours, the more dominant the male is and in any of these territorial displays the brighter colour male almost always wins. A submissive male often turns brown or grey. A Jackson's Chameleon that is distressed may turn almost black in colour.

Females also use colour to accept or reject a suitor or to indicate that she's already pregnant.

Life Cycle Of A Chameleon

There are four basic life stages for chameleons and it is important to understand each stage in order to become a successful Herpetoculturist. These are:

1 Pre-birth/Embryonic
2 Juvenile/Sub-adult
3 Sexually Mature Adult
4 Old Age

Let's look at each in turn.

Pre-Birth/Embryonic

This should only really concern you if you are a breeder of chameleons and owners should not need to worry about this stage at all. However, it's included here in case you wish to breed your chameleons and also as it's the beginning of the life cycle. Breeders should understand and practice proper management including ensuring that females are provided with good nutrition and the housing conditions are suitable as these factors will have an impact on the health of the baby chameleons.

Juvenile/Sub-adult

This is characterized by the small size of the creature followed by rapid growth. At this stage the chameleon's main priority is to grow, which means they will mainly be concerned with food. As an owner you should provide them with as much food as they can eat but of course ensure they are getting a varied and nutritional diet.

Aggression amongst others of its own kind and territorial behaviors won't yet be an issue so it is possible to keep more than one in an enclosure, which is good news for a breeder if their Jackson's Chameleon gives birth to thirty babies. However, any larger animals will have a competitive advantage over the smaller ones and will eventually end up intimidating them, which will cause stress to both creatures, so this arrangement shouldn't be indefinite. Please don't make the mistake that a lot of owners do in believing that because two babies were born at the same time and kept in the same enclosure they can continue living this way for the rest of their lives because it just isn't true. One will always dominate the other, significantly reducing the life span of both and, as mentioned above, if they get into a territorial fight using their horns as weapons, this can result in serious injury and possibly even death.

Sexually Mature Adult

By this stage they will have reached a size where they can successfully reproduce therefore growth rate slows because their body now focuses its energy resources on reproduction rather than growth, particularly with females. Owners need to be aware of this change because excessive feeding at this stage can cause over obesity in both sexes. This is the stage where you need to monitor and reduce food intake and supplementation.

This is also the time where these creatures become territorial and show aggressive and defensive displays as well as developing aggressive behavior. Any chameleons previously housed together now need to be separated and kept out of sight of each other.

Old Age

Sadly, many Jackson's Chameleons in captivity won't reach this life stage at all. If it is attained it is characterized by reduced feeding and limited activity. To extend the chameleon's life span at this age, owners should reduce the amount of food they provide as well as reducing the calories in their diet by providing less treats.

Although some people don't concern themselves with the life stages of their chameleon I think that it's helpful for a good owner and/or breeder to understand each one in order to monitor their animal(s) and make adjustments to their feeding schedule and their chameleon's environment in order to successfully accommodate the changes each life stage brings. This can greatly extend the life of the captive chameleon.

Chapter 2: Before You Buy

You may have your heart set on an exotic pet, maybe you've seen a Jackson's Chameleon on television and heard that they are hardy and therefore is the best one to choose. Before you go running off to the pet store there are a few things you need to know in order to decide whether or not a Jackson's Chameleon is suitable for you.

Is A Jackson's Chameleon For Me?

Do Jackson's Chameleons Make Good Pets?
The simple answer to this is yes! They are beautiful, fascinating creatures and if you like reptiles then they can be excellent pets.

However a word of warning here – chameleons are very high maintenance and they are not something to be purchased on impulse as they require a great deal of resources and dedication. A Jackson's Chameleon isn't as hardy as some other chameleon species and don't tolerate high temperatures, therefore they're not recommended for novices and if you've never owned a reptile before it is advised you choose something else first like a Corn Snake, Bearded Dragon or a Gecko until you have more experience. Having said that, they're not the most difficult exotic creature to keep and as long as you do your research and know what to expect and how to care for them properly you can raise these creatures successfully.

Important note: I do have friends who have very calm, docile Jackson's Chameleons but, like humans, chameleon's temperaments can differ therefore what I say about the characteristics in this book does not apply to ALL Jackson's Chameleons.

Before buying any sort of chameleon please think about what you are looking for in a pet. If you want an animal that you can take out and play with or teach tricks to then this creature is definitely not for you. They're not companion animals like cats and dogs, in fact they're not very sociable at all. Handling of any sort can cause them a lot of stress and they're more a "look and observe" creature like fish, rather than a playful one. For this reason they are not suitable for young children or those who want something they can touch and pick up and play with all the time.

Jackson's Chameleons do better alone and although you can keep a male and a female together for breeding purposes, once they've been bred the pair should always be separated again. Two males together is a definite no-no. Even being kept in separate cages can cause them to display aggressive behaviour if they can see each other, which can cause unnecessary stress and lead to injury. Females are less territorial but it is recommended that you only ever keep one of these creatures at any one time. If this seems cruel then remember that they are solitary and territorial creatures and even in the wild it is very rare that two males (or females for that matter) would voluntarily remain within sight of each other, other than when breeding. The difference is that in the wild they have as much space as they could possibly need to escape each other whereas in captivity they won't.

Some households are inappropriate for these creatures. Those with children under five, pregnant women, elderly people or anyone with a compromised immune system shouldn't be keeping this type of pet. Partly because of the risk of disease transmission but also because they need a quiet household as well as a dedicated owner willing to spend a lot of time to take care of them.

So why are they so difficult?
In captivity a lot of chameleons don't live past eighteen months. To raise them successfully you need to understand how they live in the wild. They spend most of their time in treetops, soaking up direct sunlight and eating a wide variety of insects. Jackson's Chameleons

come from countries with large amounts of rainfall per year and which are naturally humid environments.

The biggest challenges are to ensure a full spectrum of lighting, warm temperatures with high humidity levels, plenty of water and a good mixture of suitable insects.

You may read that the Jackson's Chameleon was one of the first types of chameleons to be kept successfully in captivity and this may give the impression that it is hardy and easy to look after. Whilst some owners do manage to raise Jackson's Chameleons for a long time, how long they live is dependent upon the owner and how much they know about the species as well how good their setup is. If they are purchased on a whim without the necessary equipment they will not live very long. They need a specialist environment as close to the conditions wild chameleons would experience therefore you need to be prepared and do a lot of research on their care requirements.

For these reasons, the Jackson's Chameleon is more suited for someone who has successfully raised other breeds of chameleons. If this is your first it may be wiser to try keeping a Veiled or a Panther Chameleon first. That said, they aren't impossible for novices, it will just take a lot more research in order to understand their needs.

Cost To Purchase
You've got your heart set on a Jackson's Chameleon. I guess whether they're expensive or not depends on your definition of the word 'expensive'. In the UK you can purchase a Jackson's Chameleon for around £199 (in the US that equates to around $262) depending on the species and where you purchase it from: online prices, for instance, may be less expensive than a pet shop. Whilst some people may gulp at the price, given that it is an exotic pet, I don't think that this is too bad for a creature you truly love.

I will note here that Jackson's Chameleons are incredibly hard to get hold off. This is because they are so delicate they need excellent care requirements in order to live past four or five months which means only dedicated breeders are willing to take the chance and breed them. As there is a large population in Hawaii, in America you can buy a Jackson's Chameleon for as low as $24.99 but these are wild caught animals and are not recommended, firstly because they don't adapt well to captive conditions and secondly because you don't really know what medical problems it may have.

Let's imagine you can find a reputable breeder and you are considering purchasing a Jackson's Chameleon. The price above is simply that of purchasing it, keeping it is another matter.

Set up requires a large cage, the larger the better, add in the plants, lighting and heating and it can be a costly affair. Then you have food plus any items that need to be replaced after six months or so such as the light bulbs. The following is a rough estimate of the cost of setting up and keeping a Jackson's Chameleon. (Please note prices were correct at the time of going to press - although these can change according to currency fluctuations which, of course is out of the author's control).

Set Up Costs
Jackson's Chameleon - £199 ($262)
Vivarium - £160+ ($216)
Plants - £50-£100+ ($81-135) (depending on if they're artificial or real)

Lighting
UVB light bulb £18.99+ ($25+)
Light fixtures and stands - £70+ ($94+)
Basking Lamp - £29.99+ ($40+)
Basking light bulbs £15.49 (Pack of two) ($21+)

Reflector - £8.79+ ($12+)
Timer for Lights - £6.99+ ($9+)
Digital Hygrometer for temperature and humidity - £6.79+ ($9+)
Heat Guard - £10.69+ ($14.50+)

Watering
Hand spray bottle £1.99+ ($2.70+)
Drippers (basic) £7.99+ ($10.82+)
Automatic Mister £39.99+ ($54.16+)

Food (Approximately a months worth)
Baby Chameleon
Flightless Fruit Flies - £3.83 ($5.19)
Small crickets £2.81 ($3.81)
Mini mealworms £8.95 ($12.12)

Adult Chameleon
Crickets - £2.81 ($3.81)
Waxworms - £2.45($3.32)
Mealworms - £8.95 ($12.12)
Butterworms - £6.60 ($8.94)
Dubia Roaches - £3.50 ($4.74)
Locusts - £4.20 ($5.69)

Containers for insects - £11.99 each ($16.24)
Cost to gut-load food – Approx. £20+ per month ($27+)

Supplements
Phosphorous Free Calcium With Vitamin D3 - £8.19 ($11.09)
Phosphorous Free Calcium Without Vitamin D3 - £7.05 ($9.60)

Vet Bills
Dependent on area - £15+ consultation ($20+)
Operations or medicines - £30+ ($40+)

Okay so let's say I buy a Jackson's Chameleon for around £199 ($262). If I then add everything on the above list spending £60 ($79) on plants and choosing an automatic mister instead of an ordinary hand spray bottle then it would come to around £670.47 ($884.32).

If I decided to buy 6 insect containers at £11.99 then this would come to another £71.94 making a grand total of £742.41 (Around $979.20). Yes, I could make this slightly cheaper by taking off the automatic mister and using a hand spray bottle and using margarine tubs instead of insect containers and I probably don't need a light timer but if we're looking at the optimal set up this is about the cheapest you could do it for. Bear in mind that the £160 is for the smallest cage you could possibly keep your Jackson's Chameleon in and the cost of food is based on if you had around four different types of insects and you spend a pound a week on vegetables and fruit for gut-loading – this could be more or less dependent on where you shop and the prices in your area. Realistically you would probably be looking at around £200 ($270.89) upwards for a good sized vivarium which would then increase your plant costs. Plus, if you're buying from pet shops or breeders rather than over the Internet then your prices could be slightly increased again. Lighting costs will vary depending on how you set them up but all in all you're looking at least £750 ($989) upwards to set up and buy your Jackson's Chameleon.

Not too bad you may be thinking but how much will it cost you to keep this chameleon for over a year?

Okay so once you have perfected their environment you probably won't need to keep buying more plants, other than one every now and then if one dies and your light fittings should only need to be bought once. If you buy a baby chameleon you may opt for a smaller cage in which case you would have to replace it once your chameleon has outgrown it but this would then be a one off cost.

So far so good but there are monthly costs and items that will need to be replaced at least once, if not twice throughout the year such as the basking and heat light bulbs, food (both insects for the chameleon and food used for gut-loading those insects) and supplements as well as a vet check-up once a year.

Taking these into account, assuming you spend around £50 on food items a month, replace your supplements and lights twice a year and have a very basic vet check once a year, you could be looking at around £695 ($941) a year to keep your Jackson's Chameleon healthy and happy. This is assuming it never needs an operation or medication.

Yes this is a very broad estimate - your Jackson's Chameleon may not eat such a variety of food or may eat less than what I've estimated here, you may shop around and find cheaper products, your vet could cost more or less than what I have estimated, et cetera. I feel I have probably been generous with the pricing and you will be looking at more but basically the takeaway from here is they're not cheap and you need to weigh up whether these costs are worth it or not before jumping in and buying one.

With regards to cost I would give you three pieces of advice –

The first is if you really have your heart set on one of these beautiful creatures then you should buy a little bit of equipment each week or month (depending on what you can afford) and set everything up over time. Not only does this spread the cost but it also gives you time to research the perfect environment and husbandry techniques. I do feel that if you are putting in a time commitment and buying things a little bit here and there that you are also clearly serious about owning one rather than buying on a whim.

My second piece of advice would be to price up what it costs to insure your Jackson's Chameleon. Yes, they may never get sick and it might not be worth your while but if you're a novice owner there is a higher chance your chameleon could become ill and you would need to see the vet and these visits often aren't cheap, especially if they prescribe medication or say your pet needs an operation. It may not be worthwhile doing but I do think it's worth researching.

The third piece of advice would be to maybe look at reducing your food costs by raising your own insect colonies. This may not be an option for you if you are squeamish – although let's get this straight now, your Jackson's Chameleon NEEDS live insects to stay healthy. If you're squeamish then it probably isn't the right pet for you at all. Some people don't like the noises the crickets and some other insects make but if you're going to be keeping any sort of chameleon then it could be a good idea.

Breeding kits range from around £9.50 -£17.99 (Approximately $12-24) upwards depending on what type of insects you're breeding and where you buy them from. You can buy a variety of kits such as crickets, mealworms, waxworms, locusts and so on. Don't forget you will need to feed these animals as well so your cost of gut-loading will increase and you will need to maintain these insects properly such as cleaning out their containers and replenishing their food daily, removing any insects that have died and so on. It isn't for everyone but is something worth thinking about.

Ideally your Jackson's Chameleon could live up to ten years so you need to weigh up the costs and decide if you could afford to keep them for this long. Are you prepared for this type of cost commitment?

Where To Buy

When purchasing a chameleon there are usually a few options available, all of which have advantages and disadvantages, for instance there are good and bad pet shops just as there are good and bad breeders and good and bad owners. Whichever method you choose is entirely up to you and you need to make your own mind up about whether you are purchasing from someone who is reputable or not although as mentioned above, you may be limited as to where you buy with a Jackson's Chameleon, especially in the UK.

NEVER be pressurised into buying and NEVER buy a chameleon because you feel sorry for it or because you are so excited and desperate to own one. If you end up buying one that has been mistreated or is already ill then chances are no matter how perfect your set up is, it will die.

The following are the main options for buying –

Pet Shop
I hear a lot of people saying these are a no-no when it comes to exotic pets, especially chameleons.
"They don't take care of them properly."
"They're poorly housed and maintained."
Yes there may be pet shops like these who stock these creatures without knowing how to care for them. I've never been to a pet shop that only has one sort of pet with each one kept in separate cages where they can't see each other; this being a major requirement for a chameleon. However I can't tar all pet shops with the same brush. Some are specialists in exotic pets and these are the best ones to go to. Usually they're small and local rather than big chains so may be slightly more expensive but the advantages of buying from them are you can talk to people and ask their advice about the animal and the vivarium. A good pet shop will know a lot about the creatures and

will be able to answer pretty much every question you have. Usually they'll be enthusiastic and willing to talk to you and share their knowledge and experience.

Another advantage is if you are sold a sick chameleon you have somebody to hold accountable as you can return to a pet shop or put in a complaint.

You can also see the chameleon in person, where and how it's been kept and check its health before you buy. You can also ask about its feeding habits, age, sex and where it was sourced from.
The disadvantage is that pet shops, no matter how good, aren't ideal environments for chameleons and they may be sick purely because of the conditions they are kept under. The owners or workers may be keener on making money than they are about the creature's well-being and they may try and sell you a whole load of things that aren't suitable or even necessary.

The best way to avoid this is to do your research so you know what to be alert for and to know the right questions to ask and what the right answers should be.

Reptile Fair
These are great as you will have both pet shops and breeders available and there will be so many creatures to choose from. However in this setting it's not possible to see how they have been raised or housed.

The good news is you will be able to talk to people directly and ask about their experience with exotic pets. Usually the people attending these types of fairs are very knowledgeable and again you will be able to check the health of the chameleons for yourself.

Always ask for the contact information of a seller so you can ask questions later if you need to and again, so that you have someone to hold accountable should anything go wrong.

The downside of these fairs is that the person you buy from will usually live far away so it's not feasible to go there for advice or to buy supplies once you have made a purchase.

Breeder

Okay so I said I wasn't going to recommend a particular option but this is by far my favourite, especially for a Jackson's Chameleon where it is difficult to raise the babies. You read and research and then you book an appointment with a professional breeder with a reputation for producing healthy animals. If you're searching online then by all means check any reviews that have been posted to see what other people think of them but be aware that these aren't always trustworthy – most people will only post a review if they've had a bad experience and of course people known to the breeder could post false reviews.

The reason why this is one of the best options is you can see how the chameleons have been raised and kept. You can ask questions and get an idea of whether the breeder is being honest with you as well as how knowledgeable and experienced they are.
If you don't like the set up or the look of the chameleons then you don't buy but usually this isn't the case, as in order to have a good reputation as a breeder you usually have to be an expert with keeping these creatures healthy. Anyone who doesn't have the expertise will not be able to keep the offspring alive in order to sell them anyway. Also, if a breeder is inviting you into their home they're most likely proud of their set up and willing for you to inspect it. Not only that, a responsible breeder may interrogate you as to your set up and knowledge of these creatures. Don't be offended if this happens, instead see it as a good sign – clearly if they're worried about the

type of home the babies are going to then they must love these creatures and aren't in it just for money.

The advice of these breeders is like gold – they can tell you the brands of the lamps they use, where they buy their supplies, the type of calcium supplement and food the chameleons have been eating and even how often they eat and poop. As these chameleons are being raised as pets they will most likely have handled them from a young age and will be able to show you how to do this properly. They may also have an idea of each one's temperament.
You still need to do your homework though and don't just rely on the information purely from one owner but if you do this before visiting you should be pretty confident about whether or not the breeder is trustworthy and safe to buy from. Of course the downside to buying from breeders is that you may have to travel quite far in order to visit which means you may be more tempted to buy there and then.

Private Seller
Unlike a breeder who is raising chameleons from birth in order to sell them on, private sellers are mostly people who have bought a chameleon but are selling it on because they can't – or won't – take care of them.

These can be healthy and properly cared for but you need to ask yourself - why is this person selling? It may be that they have purchased the Jackson's Chameleon and then realised, too late, the amount of work it involves and have realised they don't have the time or the expertise to care for it. It may be because they are moving away and can't take it with them for whatever reason or maybe they've changed jobs and know they won't have as much time for it. However, there are also those people that have realised that the chameleon isn't healthy, possibly because they lack understanding of how to care for it properly. Sorry if I sound condescending here but let's face it, it's not fun taking care of a sick animal that needs pricy medical attention, so most people in this situation would want to sell it on as quickly as possible.

A responsible owner who wants a good home for their beloved pet will be willing to help you assess the health of the chameleon. They will have kept good records of its food, cage temperatures, humidity levels and health and should be willing to let you go to their house and check it out should you wish to do so.

Another advantage of buying this way is that the private seller may be selling the vivarium, lighting and all the other equipment that goes with it. You can find some good deals on the Internet for the whole set up from around £200 ($263.79).

The downside of this is that, again, an owner may be far from where you live. An owner may offer for you to visit them and then they will deliver it if you wish to buy it, giving them an opportunity to check out the living arrangements you will be providing the creature with. These would be the best type of people to buy from because again, they clearly love their pet enough to check out its potential new home.

Internet
This can be private owner, pet shop or breeder, shipping to you. It's by far the quickest and easiest option. You can read information from their websites, ask questions via email and see photographs. You don't have to travel far – or at all – and you can buy, pay and ship overnight.

I have to say this, for me, is the worst possible way to buy any chameleon but especially as one as sensitive as the Jackson's. You don't know where the exotic pet is coming from, how it's raised or housed or what its health is like and you're now also adding the trauma of shipping into the mix.

Your questions are being answered by a faceless, unknown person who could just be telling you what you want to hear and how do you even know the picture you have seen is of the chameleon you are buying? Who is held accountable if something goes wrong or you have a complaint?

Wherever you buy from always choose a captive bred chameleon as wild ones often carry parasites and disease, which mean they may already be sick or getting sick by the time they reach you. These creatures are delicate enough and don't need the stress of being caught plus they find it very difficult to adapt to captive conditions, which will make it even harder for you to keep them alive.
In many countries it is illegal to capture and transport wild chameleons so buy purchasing one you are supporting a trade where many animals die horrible, slow deaths before they even reach the pet store or new owner.

Instead, if you choose not to buy from a breeder directly, look for ethically sourced chameleons; those that have been captive bred and properly raised, even though this may be difficult to find. The best place to look is on forums or social media sites dedicated to chameleons as there may be breeders using those sites who will advertise when their babies have been born and are ready to be sold.

What To Look For

As chameleons are incredibly difficult to look after it is very important that you have a healthy one to start with. They should have a smooth, even body with no sign of mites. It is very difficult to assess if a chameleon is sick because they are wild animals and as such are adept at hiding illness or injury as these would make them a target for predators in the wild but there are some indicators you can look for.

Signs Of A Healthy Chameleon

- Full, smooth, rounded, even body.
- Strong, even, smooth jawline.
- Fat, rounded tail.

Always be sure to check the following -

Eyes – These should be clear and bright, bulging and turret like in appearance not cloudy or sunken and should be actively moving about as the lizard views its surroundings, especially as you approach it.

Mouth – Look for an irregular jawline or dents in the mouth without a cottage cheese like substance known as mouth rot.

Body – If you can see the chameleon's ribs or hip bones protruding then it is most likely undernourished. Look for open wounds, bite marks, swollen toes or a limp, as these are indicators that the chameleon has been injured. Red, fluid filled patches can indicate thermal burns. The chameleon's body should be brightly coloured and not dull unless it's in shed and although they are naturally slow creatures they should still be active and have a good strong grip on the branches and twigs.

Faeces – Not the greatest thing to inspect but if there's any evidence of loose unhealthy stools or there are faeces smeared at the animal's anal opening then this is another sign that it could have a health condition.

Mites – These are reddish brown spots around the mouth, eyes and ear area.

Questions To Ask

Is The Chameleon Wild Caught Or Captive Bred? – You should NEVER buy a wild caught chameleon. These often carry parasites and can have other medical issues. Not only that but they don't tend to live as long as they find it difficult to adapt to captivity.

Can I See The Animal's Health Records? - It is very important to keep a journal for each animal that records feeding, instances of refusing feeds, defecation, shedding and unusual behaviour or changes in behaviour along with the dates of bulb changes. This not only helps the owner to monitor their chameleon and flag up any signs of ill health but also helps the vet troubleshoot health issues.

When buying a chameleon you should ask to check these records, especially if you're buying a second hand pet.

When Was The Last Physical Examination? – This applies more to older chameleons, and again this is especially important from private sellers but it can also apply to younger chameleons and breeders. For an exotic pet like this they should have regular physical exams, at least once a year.

How Old Is The Chameleon? – Avoid buying very young chameleons under three months old unless you are a very experienced keeper. Under three months and they're usually not ready to move to a new home, their feeding habits won't yet be established and it won't always be clear if they have any health defects or not.

How Often Is The Chameleon Handled? – If you are buying from a private seller or a pet shop the answer could well be never. This is fine, after all, chameleons don't enjoy being handled and I would never recommend you do this, they are a merely to be enjoyed by watching. You would never pull a tropical fish from a tank so why would you want to cuddle your chameleon? However, if you buy from a breeder who handles them from very young the chameleons can get used to it. Having a Jackson's Chameleon you can pick up every now and then without causing too much stress can be handy if, for example, you want to take them outside or you want to free range them for exercise or if you need to take them to the vet.

What Does The Chameleon Eat? – The answer to this will probably be crickets (for babies it should be pinhead crickets and wingless fruit flies) but if you ask what else they've been given it can give you an idea of its favourite treats as well as the feeders it doesn't like. Knowing this can help you settle your chameleon quicker and is advantageous if you are trying to handle them as you can offer something they enjoy. Also, a chameleon *should* be given a variety of different foods so this will help you determine whether they are being provided a healthy, nutritious diet – if you are buying an adult chameleon who only has a diet of crickets then this signals that they aren't getting a balanced diet and therefore may have health problems as a result of this.

What Is The Chameleon's Temperament Like? – Knowing this will give you an idea of whether you should handle the chameleon or not. If you are buying a laid back juvenile from a breeder that handles it every day then this gives an indication that you would be okay to handle it every now and then. If you are buying, say, an older chameleon or one that shows signs of stress whenever somebody comes near, then handling it will be a no-no and if you are buying a chameleon you can take out and pet then this probably won't be suitable for you.

Why Are You Selling? – Of course this question is redundant if you're buying from a breeder or a pet shop as the reason is obvious – they want to make money and in the case of breeders, they have too many chameleons and need to get rid of them. However this is more for if you are buying from a private seller, especially if they've only had them a short while. The answer may be that they're moving away or they've changed jobs and aren't home as much or maybe they've bought the chameleon without realising how much work and time it takes to look after them. Of course they may not tell you the truth – I doubt very much anyone would say "oh I haven't looked after it properly and it's going to cost me an extortionate amount in vet bills to make it healthy again" but hopefully if you speak over the telephone or, even better, in person, you will be able to get a measure of the person and decide whether they are being honest or not. If you meet in person you should also have the chance to examine the Jackson's Chameleon, see its habitat and get an idea of whether it's healthy or not.

If you are buying an older, second hand chameleon I would also recommend you ask how long the person has owned it. You may well be buying a two year old Jackson's Chameleon and assume that the person selling has had it since it was a baby and this may not necessarily be the case – maybe they purchased it from somebody else when it was eighteen months or a year old. I wouldn't recommend buying a chameleon that has been passed from person to person as you cannot determine what its life has been like or how it's been kept in each home.

Chapter 3: Vivarium

You should always ensure your housing is set up before you bring home your chameleon. Not only will it make it easier for your new friend to settle in (where would you keep it if you didn't have a vivarium?) but also allows you to get it to the correct temperature and humidity beforehand and therefore hopefully avoid any health issues.

Size

As stated previously, although compared to some other chameleon breeds, a Jackson's Chameleon needs a lot of space. They're arboreal creatures, which means they love to be high up in the trees. The advantage of this is that the cage needs to be taller than it is wide so it doesn't necessarily need to take up a lot of room, a corner would suffice but remember the bigger the cage the better.

The recommended minimum size for an adult is 24 inches (width) x 24 inches (depth) x 36 inches (height) (61cm x61cm x 90 cm). If you can make it bigger then I beg you to do so. A real bugbear of mine is seeing people posting pictures of their enclosures on the Internet that look far too small for their chameleon. Whilst it is true that the Jackson's Chameleon is one of the smaller breeds of chameleon they still climb and like to move about so the taller and wider the better.

This is a good time to point out that a lot of people are buying cages that are classed as 'large' by the retailers but are in fact too short and doesn't give them enough room to climb. Through no fault of their own, otherwise conscientious owners are putting their chameleons in unsuitable enclosures. Take care to ensure that you are buying a cage specifically for a Jackson's Chameleon and not for reptiles in general.

It is recommended that if you are purchasing a baby then you start off with a smaller enclosure and if you can spare the extra expense there are advantages to this as it makes eating, drinking and basking less strenuous for the chameleon. If you don't want to spend money on something that is going to only last a short time then you can put a baby chameleon in an adult cage if they are healthy but as they can easily become lost and may find it difficult to catch food then they will need to be monitored closely. Of course a bigger cage will make monitoring slightly more difficult as there will be more places to hide.

Whatever you choose to do remember that height needs to be a priority and you should place your cage on a table or cupboard or some other stable surface rather than putting it onto the floor. Remember your Jackson's Chameleon, although a pet to you is first and foremost a wild animal and a very territorial one at that. It will most likely view you, your family and any other pets as predators and will feel far more comfortable high up. It should be at least above eye level but as far as your chameleon is concerned the higher you can get them the better.

Caging Material
The cages you can buy can be made of glass, screen (or mesh) or even wood and there are pros and cons for all of these. The main things to consider when choosing are ventilation, temperature and humidity so we will look at each one of these in turn.

Ventilation - If your cage isn't properly ventilated then the air will become stale which can cause respiratory problems. Not only that but stagnant air can also allow fungus and bacteria to grow, again leading to health problems and could potentially result in your chameleon dying.

The good news is screen cages are readily available and less expensive than glass, not only that but they offer good ventilation. When I talk about 'glass' I'm not talking about an aquarium. I hear many people say "oh I have an old fish tank I'm going to put my chameleon in". These are not suitable as not only are they not tall enough they don't provide enough ventilation. A glass cage will need a screen or mesh door or ceiling with a fan blowing across the top of the cage which is placed on the outside not the inside.

Humidity - Whilst a screen cage is excellent for ventilation it's not so good for humidity. This is where choosing suddenly becomes more difficult as you need to consider the climate that you live in. If you are in an environment that is humid a screen cage is probably the perfect choice but if you live in a dry, arid area, glass may be better as it is easier to manipulate humidity levels if there is less exposure to air outside the cage. Jackson's Chameleons need around 60-80% humidity levels so you need to take this into consideration when choosing your new lizard's habitat.

Heat

A wooden or glass cage will retain heat, making it easier to control the temperature but again, both need good ventilation to allow the air to circulate, whereas a screen cage will lose heat. The location of your chameleon's home will be a key factor; is it indoors or outdoors? Do you live in a hot, humid environment or a cold one? For instance, if your chameleon cage is going to be indoors and your home is around 22-24 degrees Celsius (72-75 degrees Fahrenheit) then a screen enclosure with a single lamp could be sufficient enough to provide your Jackson's Chameleon with the temperature range it requires, whereas in the same conditions a glass cage may overheat. In comparison, in cooler climates a screen cage may not be hot enough even with lamps.

Buying a cage therefore isn't as easy as one might think. Glass, wood and mesh are all good options but it is not possible to recommend one over the other without knowing the environment you live in. The best way to choose is to consider the climate your home offers compared to the climate your chameleon requires and decide which enclosure will best meet its needs.

The other option of course is to build your own. The advantage to this is you have the ability to create either a grand masterpiece to be a focal point in the room or a simple, functional habitat in the corner. If you do choose to build your own remember to plan first. The needs of your chameleon should always be top of the list. There's no point making an elaborate cage that looks wonderful if your chameleon can escape or is too cold.

Also consider your budget and skill-set. If you've never built anything in your life this route may not be suitable. A few pieces of wood nailed haphazardly together could end up being more of a danger than a sanctuary for your new pet.

If you do decide on custom made then be thoughtful and cautious when choosing materials. For instance, glass is expensive and difficult to work with, plastic can melt in high heat and wood can rot if not treated properly.

Always remember, whichever type of cage you choose, the top must ALWAYS be a screen. This is because UVB will not penetrate glass or plastic and this is an important requirement for your Jackson's Chameleon.

Make sure it's escape proof and fits snugly on the tank with strong clips locking it on.

Whichever type of enclosure you choose it is wise to have it set up BEFORE you bring your chameleon home. Yes, I know I've already said this several times but it is an important rule that potential owners should adhere too. Once it's completed you can keep an eye on humidity, ventilation and temperature before your new pet is exposed to it. This will get you used to checking and adjusting all of these requirements regularly, giving you a better chance of providing a suitable environment that your chameleon will thrive in.

Plants And Branches

Jackson's Chameleons are arboreal creatures, meaning they seek shelter in the uppermost branches and treetops. Lots of leaves to hide amongst will make your new friend feel secure. A lot of people worry that if they put a lot of foliage in the cage their Jackson's Chameleon will hide away and they won't ever see them. I know people who have kept their cages practically bare for this very reason and guess what? Their chameleon had a very short (and unhappy) life span. Keeping them in unsuitable conditions is cruel. They are incredibly sensitive creatures and get stressed very easily. First and foremost you are creating a habitat and not an exhibition cage.

This is also a misconception. Yes, your Jackson's Chameleon will hide BUT once they settle in and feel safe they will start to come out and walk along vines and bask more. If you provide a suitable basking area using branches and a platform underneath the basking light you will be able to see your chameleon whilst he uses this area. You should also have secure perches at different levels and temperatures within the cage.

As well as lots of leaves to hide in, your enclosure will also need lots of sturdy branches, varying in length and diameter for your chameleon to walk across. Not only does this give them exercise but their feet are shaped to cling to branches and they dislike walking on flat surfaces. You can buy 'jungle vines' in some pet shops or garden centres. Make sure the plants you use give adequate support. Remember your chameleon should be able to easily navigate the whole enclosure.

You can use fake plants and in some cases these may be preferred as they are easy to clean. However, real plants will help increase and maintain humidity and are better at holding water droplets for drinking which is important as chameleons don't tend to recognise standing water and therefore won't drink it.

The most common ones to use are Pothos, Hibiscus, Umbrella Plants, Dracaenia, Aloe, Spider plants and Philodendrens, which are all reptile safe. A lot of people will recommend Ficus too but these excrete a white milky latex which is mildly toxic and has been connected to a number of eye infections in chameleons, therefore it may be one to avoid, especially with a Jackson's Chameleon which tends to be more sensitive anyway. Research each plant you put in beforehand to make sure that you only choose non-toxic ones as well as those that won't die in high humidity.

Be careful about bringing in plants and branches from outside as these can carry parasites that could cause your chameleon to become ill.

The plants DO NOT need to be near a window, as they will thrive under the lighting in your chameleon's cage.

Substrate
This is simply the material that is used to line the bottom of the cage, also known by some as 'bedding. The most popular ones for Jackson's Chameleons are topsoil, peat, moss or coconut fibre. These should be kept moist but not too wet or soggy. Be aware that if the bedding is moist but the enclosure doesn't have the proper

ventilation then the substrate will likely grow mould and mildew and this will be bad for your chameleon's health.

Substrate is a controversial topic and one that nobody appears to agree upon. A lot of people will say don't use anything as it's not necessary. Instead lining the bottom of the cage with newspaper or paper towels is a better option, as it is easier to take out and replace.

The reasons people give in favour of substrate is that it looks a lot nicer. My reply to this is that if you're a novice and are simply buying it for aesthetic reasons I would discourage you from doing so for the following reasons:

- A substrate can be easily ingested accidentally when the chameleon is catching prey and can get stuck in the digestive tract causing a blockage that could be potentially fatal. If not fatal it could cost a lot in vet bills!

- Substrate such as moss or soil is a breeding ground for bacteria and is harder to clean than newspaper that can just be gathered up and changed.

- Food can hide in the substrate making it harder to catch, especially for young ones.

To make the vivarium look nicer you could use smooth black river stones instead.

Rather than using substrate on the floor of their cage a lot of people put their plants in pots and put these into the cage. Many people will say that this is suitable as Jackson's Chameleons, tree dwellers by nature, rarely come down from the branches anyway.

If you do decide to use substrate make sure it's one that is non-toxic and easy to clean and offer food in a clean tub to avoid the risk of ingesting the substrate. Watch your chameleon closely whilst feeding and catch any insects that escape so your chameleon isn't tempted to scurry down to the bottom of the tank after them.

Don't use soil from outside as these can harbour germs and parasites that are harmful to these sensitive animals.

Lighting

This is incredibly important to your chameleons. What may appear to be nothing more than a simple lightbulb to you is actually a necessity that your Jackson's Chameleon is physically dependent upon. Bodily functions such as thermoregulation, calcium absorption and even the ability to see will require a spectrum of lighting. How much in depth knowledge you have about these lights is crucial to your success as a chameleon owner.

UVB Bulbs – These are critical. Ultraviolet-B – or UVB – is present in sunlight and the majority of animals on Earth will have some level of exposure to it but reptiles have a particular need for UVB. We humans absorb UVB and if someone has low Vitamin D levels a doctor will often recommend they sit out in the sun. Jackson's Chameleons are no different. They absorb Vitamin D from the sunlight and convert this to Vitamin D3. No D3 means calcium cannot be utilised in their system.

This can lead to the chameleon gradually developing physical problems such as stunted growth, soft eggs (in females) and recent studies have also linked lack of UVB to poor immune system. A leading killer in the reptile industry is Metabolic Bone Disease (MBD) where the chameleon's bones slowly deteriorate, eventually becoming brittle and malformed. It's incredibly painful yet can be easily avoided by fitting a UVB lightbulb.

A common mistake people make is they go off and buy the strongest UVB bulb they can find, after all these creatures live out in the desert and are constantly in the sunlight out in the wild, right? However, too much UVB can be harmful and over exposure can shorten life-span. Like everything else when it comes to the Jackson's Chameleon, the right balance is the key. Medium levels should be sufficient for most type of cages so make sure to check it is suitable before purchasing.

UVA Bulbs

Whilst this doesn't contribute to the life span of the chameleon it does affect their ability to see so I believe it is in the creature's best interest to include it here.

It is thought that reptiles can detect a larger spectrum of lighting than us mere humans can so although UVA is invisible to us, without it your Jackson's Chameleon's vision can be impaired. Some scientists have compared it to colour blindness whilst some say not providing it is akin to forcing the chameleon to live its life in a darkened room and it is thought that it affects appetite and reproduction. The importance of UVA light is still under investigation and many people are sceptical but others believe owners are neglecting the psychological well-being of these animals by not including it.

I'll let you make your own mind up but my point of view is if you want to create a perfect environment for your Jackson's Chameleon rather than just an okay, suitable for a couple of years cage then everything needs to be considered even invisible (to us) light. After all, what is the cost of a light bulb or two compared to limited vision for your beloved pet?

Basking Lights

Thermoregulation is the term used in reference to a cold blooded animals' ability to control its body temperature by moving from warmer to cooler spots. Your Jackson's Chameleon thermo-regulates manually by moving from shade to sunlight as their body temperatures change. For a complete setup a chameleon requires a basking light, which should be a hot surface in a corner near the top and will be their main source of heat.

Night
A Jackson's Chameleon must have distinct day and night periods, just like in the wild, to maintain their biological rhythms. All lights should be switched off to allow for around 12 hours of darkness with a slight drop in temperature. Their inside habitat should be reflective of an outdoor one so it is good for the daylight hours to change seasonally, however daylight periods must be light and night time periods must be dark.

The best way to ensure all the lights get switched off is to have them on a timer. Your Jackson's Chameleon's cage needs to be in a room away from any noise and light from the rest of the household so they get a sufficient amount of sleep.

Full Spectrum Bulbs
If you go into a pet shop you will see Full Spectrum Bulbs and will probably be told they're the best thing for your Jackson's Chameleon, after all it says right there on the packaging that it provides every form of light a reptile will ever need – heat, UVB, UVA and so on.

Again, these are controversial amongst chameleon owners because most compact bulbs are incapable of providing a significant amount of UVB output so choose wisely and research which best suits your enclosure before purchasing.

A UV tube may be a better option and a T5 tube is recommended as if it's attached to the ceiling with a reflector it can send UVB rays to approximately 60 centimetres (24 inches) and will last around nine months before needing to be replaced.

T8 units are also available but these only travel approximately 30 centimetres (12 inches) and will only last roughly six months. Remembering to replace your UVB lights is important so make a note of when you buy them otherwise it can be difficult to tell because although they may still switch on they may not be sending out high enough levels of UVB. They're definitely worth investing in, after all a UVB light replacement could end up being a lot cheaper than the vet fees that could result from a sick, unhappy chameleon.

All lights should be on top of the cage on the OUTSIDE shining downwards. As chameleons have a tendency to climb anything they can, keeping lights on the inside poses a risk of burns.

Gradient Temperature
For them to thermo-regulate it is essential that you provide your chameleon with a gradient of temperatures within their habitat to allow them to do this. This means it needs to be cooler on the bottom and warmer at the top so the chameleon can move in and out of the heat as it needs to. This is also why you need to provide plenty of plants for shade as the Jackson's Chameleon needs to have the means to cool itself down to prevent overheating. The temperature of the cage needs to be monitored daily using a thermometer with a probe or an infrared temperature gun if possible. You can buy stick on ones fairly cheap but these are highly inaccurate. Make sure you check the temperature in different places to ensure that there are plenty of cool spots and plenty of hot spots.

It is important to make sure you adjust the temperature if necessary otherwise your chameleon can become sick with respiratory disease.

They may also stop eating as without proper heat and light they have trouble digesting.

A guide to temperature is -
Daytime gradient of 21-26.5 degrees Celsius (70-80 degrees Fahrenheit)
Basking spot of no more than 29 degrees Celsius (85 degrees Fahrenheit)

Night time – 16.5 degrees Celsius (62 degrees Fahrenheit)

Jackson's Chameleons can tolerate a temperature drop of about 5-10 degrees Celsius (10-15 degrees Fahrenheit) at night so if they live indoors then as long as your house doesn't drop too far below 16 degrees Celsius (62 degrees Fahrenheit) then you shouldn't need to heat your chameleon's enclosure at night. A drop in temperature is necessary because is slows down their metabolism and facilitates heavy sleeping. They will not rest well at night if it's too hot.

In the morning your Jackson's Chameleon will head straight up to the basking spot, which is important as this speeds up their metabolism allowing them to hunt and digest their food properly.

Baby chameleons should be kept a bit cooler than adults during the day. 21-23 degrees Celsius (75-80 degrees Fahrenheit) should be sufficient for one that is nine months or younger. This is because younger animals aren't always good at thermoregulation and may not get out of the heat when they need to. Instead they tend to open their mouths to cool themselves down rather than moving to a different spot. If you see this with your chameleon, whatever the age, it is worth checking the temperatures and adjusting if necessary.

Jackson's Chameleons don't tolerate temperatures over 32 degrees Celsius (90 degrees Fahrenheit) very well so if you keep your chameleon outdoors and you live in a hot country be aware of over-heating and make sure you provide plenty of foliage to give them shelter from the sun and keep the overall temperature in the enclosure down.

Habitat Maintenance

Cage maintenance is an important part of keeping reptiles healthy and protecting them from harmful parasites. Every day you should spot clean your Jackson's Chameleon's cage removing any faeces, shed skin, soiled substrate (if you're using some) and uneaten food – basically anything that can go mouldy, grow bacteria or start to smell.

If you do use a substrate, sniff the cage and ensure that there is no odour of mould or mildew. If you get even the slightest whiff of this then all the substrate should be removed immediately.

Their faecal matter can carry salmonella which can be passed onto humans so be sure to thoroughly wash your hands immediately after coming into contact with your chameleon or their cage.

At least once a month you should remove everything and thoroughly clean the entire tank using a mild disinfectant. These can be bought but you should always check that they are suitable for your chameleon – I always check online to see what other owners/breeders are using –just remember to follow the instructions properly.

Wash down the cage and any 'furniture' such as the plants and stones then rinse everything off thoroughly with plain water. Once everything is clean and rinsed off put everything back in, if you can keep it as identical as possible your chameleon will be a lot happier and less stressed as they won't have to get used to new surroundings every time you clean.

If you are using a substrate then this should be changed every three months providing it hasn't gone mouldy before then. It is much harder to keep substrate clean so paper towels and newspaper may prove to be an easier and preferable option as you can pick them up and change them each day in a matter of minutes.

When you do the daily spot clean it is fine for your chameleon to stay in the cage and an advantage to this is they will get used to you opening and closing their cage door. However, when you do the deep clean your chameleon should be put in a temporary cage, out of the way of the detergents and should only be put back in when everything is thoroughly rinsed and dried off.

Chapter 4: Watering And Drainage

A common health problem with captive chameleons is dehydration. Every living creature needs water but unlike pets such as cats or dogs, keeping a Jackson's Chameleon hydrated isn't as easy as putting down a bowl of water and changing it every day. Again, successful hydration of your chameleon means understanding how they live in the wild and trying to mimic these conditions as closely as possible.

A Jackson's Chameleon comes from a place where rainfall averages approximately 30-60 inches per year. To stay hydrated a Jackson's Chameleon will lick morning dew from the leaves and soak themselves in rainfalls. Chameleons don't recognise standing water so a dirty puddle of water pooled on the floor will not entice them to drink.

Misting
The best way to simulate the natural drinking habit of a chameleon in the wild is by misting. This simply means spraying a fine mist over their cage every few hours during daylight hours only, ensuring all the plants and leaves get a good soaking. This misting is meant to mimic rain and the chameleon will then sip water droplets from the leaves. Remember some chameleons are shyer than others and you may have one that won't eat or drink in front of you, which is why real plants are sometimes better than fake ones as they tend to hold the water better.

You should also spray the chameleon itself as this will help keep them moist, making shedding easier.

Don't worry if you see your Jackson's Chameleon puffing out its bulbous eye and rubbing it on a branch. This is perfectly normal behaviour and is a way of cleaning its eyes.

The first misting session should be around one hour after you switch the lights on. Keep in mind the first thing your Jackson's Chameleon will do upon waking is head on up to their basking spot to raise their temperature. The last thing they want at this time is to be drenched in water as this can lower their body temperature. It's akin to someone throwing a bucket of water over you or dragging you under a cold shower as soon as your eyes open – not a pleasant experience. You should also allow around three or four hours each session and the final misting should be done at least two hours before you switch the lights off for the night to ensure the enclosure has time to dry out. You don't want a soggy, water logged environment for your Jackson's Chameleon as this will lead to medical problems. Again, you're imitating an environment that is humid and where dew and rain dries out pretty quickly.

One way of misting is with a spray bottle which are cheap and can be bought for around £1-£5 ($1-$5 in the US). You may even already have one lying around at home but just make sure that if you do use one you find in the cupboard that it isn't one that has ever had any chemicals in. A Jackson's Chameleon is so sensitive anyway that using a bottle that had chemicals in, even if it has been thoroughly washed out, can cause problems.

You can also mist with a pressurised spray bottle. These are slightly more expensive but tend to create a finer mist than regular spray bottles. Your chameleon may prefer being sprinkled with a light, small mist rather than the hard drenching it may get from a cheaper bottle. Most hardware or garden stores should have these pressurised water pumps, which cost anything from £10 upwards (prices start from $10 upwards in the US). Of course you can buy proper ones specially made for chameleons and reptiles in pet shops or online and these will cost you around £59.99 upwards (prices in the US start from around $63 upwards) but again you may prefer to have something more specialised so that you can be safe in the knowledge that you are using something suitable.

Now of course many of us want to keep costs down but if you are planning on buying a cheap spray bottle think how practical it is for you to hand mist. If you leave the house at 8 am, for example, you will need to mist before you go. If you decide to do this at 7.30am then you need to switch the lights on at 6.30am to give your chameleon an hour to bask. The next misting will need to be around 10.30am and again around 1.30pm. You can then get the last one in around 4.30pm giving the enclosure two hours to dry before you turn the lights out at 6.30pm so the Jackson's Chameleon can get its required twelve hours of darkness.

If you are home all day or your commute from work is fairly quick so you can come back at lunch time then you can probably do it but if you are out of the house for eight hours or more at a time then unless you have someone that can come in to your home and mist for you, you may need to invest in an automatic misting system, again these are more expensive but are reliable and convenient and could be worth the time it saves in the long run. You may read that it is acceptable to mist for five minutes twice a day and although this could be enough to keep your chameleon alive, if you want to keep a healthy Jackson's Chameleon in as perfect an environment as possible so they lead a long and happy life then you need to mist more often.

It is worth noting that there is a lot of contradictory information regarding the length of time you should mist and how often. This is because everyone's environment is different so it is all dependent upon the temperatures in your house as well as their enclosure and how thirsty your chameleon is. If your chameleon is drinking rapidly then you should continue to offer water until they slow down or stop altogether. In higher temperatures chameleons often require more water so be vigilant and observant and adjust watering times accordingly.

Water needs to be clean and free from chlorine and heavy metals. If you use tap water you will need to treat it first, a better choice therefore would be bottled or natural spring water. Do not use distilled water as this lacks the minerals your chameleon needs. Again this is another topic that people disagree on and I think this is dependent once more on the area you live in and the quality of water you have. Some say distilled should only be used because in the wild chameleons only drink rainwater and other types of water will provide too many minerals. I think if you are raising a chameleon that has been captive bred then you should ask the breeder what they have been using for all their chameleons because if they are able to breed these creatures then they no doubt have a lot of experience but it is usually just a case of adjusting supplementation to balance out the extra minerals the chameleons are getting in the water.

Chameleons don't tend to like cold water so whichever type you use should be around room temperature at minimum; the warmer it is the better. It should cool down as it sprays out but you should always check the temperature beforehand.

Be careful not to soak baby chameleons as their little nostrils can become clogged up causing them to aspirate, instead just spray the leaves of the plants around them. For babies I find it's better to mist for less time, more often.

Drippers

A dripper system provides a constant supply of fresh water into the cage throughout the day so your chameleon won't go thirsty between misting sessions. It should sit on top of the enclosure and consists of a round tub with a closable top and a nozzle to adjust the drip speed as well as a long tube from which the water drips. It is a handy product and can be bought for around £10.79 in the UK (around $10 in the US) depending on the size you want.

Some people don't buy drippers and opt instead to make their own by poking a small hole in the bottom of a container such as a plastic cup or peanut butter jar and hang this at the top of the enclosure. This is perfectly acceptable but if you do this then be sure that the water drips slowly and at a fairly regular rate rather than gushing out all at once; remember the effect you're going for is that of dew drops on leaves NOT a downpour or a swimming pool. Also ensure that you put it somewhere safe where your Jackson's Chameleon can't reach it and make sure it is secure enough that it won't fall.

You will need to put another container inside the cage to catch the drips so that your chameleon's cage doesn't become water logged. Some of the live insects you will feed your chameleon, such as crickets, are attracted to water so to prevent them from climbing in and drowning you should cover this container with a mesh sheet. This will also stop your chameleon from climbing in and injuring itself, too.

Waterfalls

This is another controversial topic but I include it in here because a lot of people think that as chameleons don't recognise standing water then a waterfall is a good solution. Look online and for every person saying "yes they look lovely and my chameleon loves drinking from it" you will find at least another three more shouting "no, don't do it, they're death traps!"

The reason they're so controversial is that a Jackson's Chameleon probably won't drink from a waterfall and so they are deemed pointless by owners. Instead, these creatures tend to defecate in them, making them a breeding ground for bacteria, which can in turn make your pet sick. Live crickets and other insects can also get caught in them and drown which could mean your chameleon gets less food than it ought to be having and they just end up looking messy.

My opinion is don't bother as your time could be better spent elsewhere but if you do decide to buy one then make sure it's kept clean and the water is draining well. I don't think it is a substitute for misting and dripping and I would always recommend these methods for providing your chameleon with water over a waterfall.

Drainage

With all this water it will only be a matter of time before your cage starts to resemble a swamp and/or overflow. Some people simply use towels at the bottom of the cage along with a container placed underneath the dripper as described above but proper drainage is better suited if you want to create an optimum enclosure as close to the wild environment as possible.

If the bottom of your cage is solid you will need to drill a hole in it. (Need I say *before* your chameleon is living there?). There are many creative ways to create drainage systems for indoor cages so it is worth looking online for ideas. Remember your cage needs to be high up so a lot of people opt for drilling holes into the bottom of the cage and then placing it on a metal shelving unit (the kind with the bars in rather than a solid shelf) with a plastic container such as a bin, directly underneath.

One person I know had a cheap chest of drawers and they drilled holes into the bottom of the cage and the top of the chest of drawers. The water drained from the cage into the top drawer, which meant they just had to pull this out to empty it.

When drilling holes be strategic and look at where the water will naturally end up so you can place the holes in the correct place.

There's no point having two drainage holes on the right hand side if the water is pooling into the middle.

Just remember, whatever sort of system you use, always remember to empty whatever container you have in place to catch water so that it doesn't overflow. The last thing you want in your lounge (or whatever room you are using) is a bin full of dirty, stagnant water.

One more thing to note is if you have holes in the bottom of your cage and you put live feeders in for your chameleon to hunt there is a risk that these insects will escape so it might be an idea to cover the bottom of the cage with a sheet of thin plastic or something similar at meal times.

Please don't ignore the importance of drainage and leave puddles of water on you cage floor. Not only will it make a mess but it will soon become dirty and lead to health issues.

Chapter 5: Feeding

Gut Loading

This means feeding the insects you are going to be giving to your Jackson's Chameleon a healthy and nutritious diet of fresh fruit and vegetables about twenty four hours before giving them to your chameleon, as these nutrients will then be passed on. For example, if you want your chameleon to get enough Vitamin A you can do this by feeding leafy green vegetables to the crickets before putting them in the cage. Although I will talk about supplements further down, most reptile veterinarians agree that gut loading is the best way to provide your chameleon the nutrients it needs, after all, in the wild the insects are not 'dusted' with vitamins and the more you can duplicate their natural habitat, the healthier and happier it will be.

Crickets, cockroaches and mealworms are easy to gut-load and should be included in your feeding plan. Crickets in particular are an ideal food source because they will devour fruits and vegetables. To gut-load you simply put the insects in a tub with fresh vegetables or fruit, leaving them for twenty four hours. Of course be careful that they have a lid on so they can't escape but this needs to be mesh or have holes so the crickets still get air, otherwise they will die.

Feeders

Jackson's Chameleons are insectivores so their diet should be comprised of insects. Again, think about how these highly specialised creatures hunt in the wild. High in the treetops of subtropical or tropical forests they are eating a wide variety of insects, both from the air and the trees all around them. You can never hope to duplicate these conditions exactly, it's impossible. For one thing the insects that you could catch is dependent upon where you live and where would you keep them all or find the time to hunt them every day? However, you should aim to get as close as possible by feeding your chameleon a variety. They will get a much more nutritional diet if you're offering four or five different insects rather than just a 'cricket only' diet, no matter how much you gut-load them first. Below is a list of the insects that these chameleons can eat in captivity.

Crickets – These are a staple of chameleon feeding because they are easy to obtain and easy to gut-load because they will eat pretty much anything. Feed the crickets fresh greens and slices of sweet potato or carrot to give them nutrition. Also provide them with a water source that won't allow them to drown such as a piece of juicy fruit or a wet sponge. Gut loaded crickets can comprise up to 80% of your chameleons total diet but they do have a low Calcium/phosphorus ratio so additional calcium supplementation should be included with most cricket meals. Supplement lightly with pure calcium powder, not one with vitamins.

You will need to feed baby and juvenile chameleons smaller crickets. Black crickets tend to bite chameleons at night so brown crickets are safer.

Please do not feed your crickets' dog food as some keepers do. By doing this not only are you missing an opportunity to add nutritional value but some dog foods contain artificial additives that can be harmful to your chameleon. (See what to avoid section below)

Locusts – These are often a great staple food because they are nutritious, have good longevity and are easy to keep. A small water source, some basic food and a plastic container at room temperature is all that is needed to keep these insects active and healthy for a number of weeks. Locusts are active and have vibrant colours making them great at arousing a resting chameleon's interest and tempting it away from its basking spot.

Dubia Roaches – A lot of owners state that these are one of the best feeder insects. Not only do their chameleons love them but they can be purchased in a variety of sizes and are also fairly cheap when bought in bulk. They are easy to breed should you wish to start your own colony. As they don't die off easily they are easy to keep until your chameleon is ready to eat them. They are much higher in protein than some other insects and the chitin shell is more digestible than that of mealworms. Whilst these roaches aren't particularly picky eaters they do prefer some foods over others so it is important that you gutload with these, remember you want them to eat as much as they possibly can so that they will be highly nutritious when you feed them to your chameleon. Good choices therefore include apples, sweet potato, squash, oranges, bananas etc. Other advantages to using Dubia Roaches as feeder insects is that they don't bite, jump or fly away, nor do they smell or make noises.

Silkworms – This is the larvae of the Silk Moth. They are good because they have a high nutritional value and are high in calcium so can be used without dusting. You can also let them develop into moths and feed these to your chameleon too.

Mealworms – These are beetle larvae and many pet stores sell them in small plastic tubs. Like crickets they can be gut loaded to increase nutritional value. However, remember to store these in the refrigerator because otherwise they will pupate and turn into beetles. "Giant mealworms" can bite so you will need to be careful how you handle them; a lot of people will squish their heads before feeding to avoid the risk of the worm biting their lizard's mouth or stomach but as most chameleons do chew these thoroughly before eating this shouldn't be a problem. They do have a high fat content though and as the hard chitin shell of the mealworm is not digestible it can cause a blockage of the gut so they should only really be given as an occasional treat and only when your Jackson's Chameleon is old enough to digest them, otherwise it can be harmful to your chameleon's health.

Waxworms (Sometimes called Grubs) – These are a type of moth larvae and can be purchased at pet stores as they are a feeder insect for a wide variety of reptiles as well as fish and birds. They are plump and waxy (hence the name), full of moisture and easy to store however they are not as nutritious as the other items on this list and, like Mealworms, have a high fat content so they shouldn't make up the chameleon's main diet. Instead they should be given now and again as a treat and to add variety. Lightly dust before feeding to increase their nutritional value.

Be aware that some chameleons love them so much they become addicted and will refuse to eat anything else. The best way to avoid this is to feed only in moderation. They are a great insect to use when hand feeding. Try to feed them when they are white in colour as this means they have shed their hard shell, which can cause blockages. You can also feed them to your chameleon when they have turned into moths.

Butterworms – These are the larvae of the Chilean Moth. They are a contrast of red and yellow in colour and apparently have a sweet buttery scent. They have high levels of calcium, which make them a great treat. However you can't gut-load them because in the wild they only eat one type of leaf, which is that of the Tebo tree. Instead you need to put them in your refrigerator, which will slow their metabolism and keep them in a hibernated state. They should also be used with caution as they have been known to cause a reaction in chameleons and whilst there is no scientific evidence to support this there are a number of cases with the same symptoms being reported and linked to these insects.

Hornworms –There are two kinds of hornworms a chameleon can eat – Tomato Hornworms and Tobacco Hornworms, named after the plants they feed on. You have them shipped to you live in little containers then feed them until they grow into large worms. If you let them pupate they will turn into Hawk Moths. If you don't mind having moths flying around you could let one or two pupate and feed them to your chameleon in moth form, they may chase it down and devour it. I've included them here because if you do an Internet search for what to feed a chameleon these are usually high on the list, however be aware that if you're in the UK/Europe they are actually banned so pet stores won't stock them. This is because they can survive and breed here, becoming a threat to the tomato industry.

Grasshoppers – These are found within the natural range of most chameleon species but you may have a harder time finding them. You don't have to feed them to your Jackson's Chameleon but as they are larger and 'meatier' than crickets they will provide a lot of nourishment. These need to be kept in a dry environment and be fed fresh greens or grass to get moisture.

Superworms or Zoophobias- Superworms look like mealworms but are far bigger and have slightly different colouring. Like crickets and mealworms they need to be fed a diet of fresh fruits and vegetables before giving them to your chameleon. What makes them better than mealworms is that there is more body than hard shell. Again you want to wait until they have just shed their hard shell and are white in colour. They are not suitable for baby or juvenile chameleons and should only be fed when your lizard is big enough to eat them.

Snails – Jackson's Chameleons are one of the few types of chameleons that will eat snails. Some owners will say they're great as their shells can contain calcium whilst others will say they are full of parasites and that their shells are hard and can have toxins. With regards to how nutritious they are this depends once again on gut-loading them correctly. Carrots, Mustard Greens, Collards and mango are all good food to give your snails. Cucumber can also be given but it's not as nutritious as dark, leafy green vegetables will be. Snails tend to be better creatures to breed rather than to buy every time for three reasons. Firstly they are difficult to get hold of, as some countries don't allow live snails to be shipped. Secondly, it is better to feed your chameleon small snails with soft shells. Thirdly, if you breed them you know they are parasite free. They are easy to breed and eggs take around three weeks to hatch and after about a month they will be a good size for your chameleon to eat.

Flies – These are included because in the wild chameleons will eat them but they don't offer as much nutrition as the insects mentioned above and as you would have to buy them from maggots, feed them until they pupate and then put them into the cage (at the risk of having them escape and buzz around your house or else remove the wings first) they are often more trouble than they're worth so many keepers skip them altogether. Flightless Fruit flies however are a great food for your baby chameleon and can be bought ready to eat.

Feeding Tips
You should always try to have at least three different feeders on hand and rotate them to stop your chameleon getting bored as they can go on a hunger strike for long periods when subjected to the same diet over and over.

Wild caught insects should not be used unless you are absolutely sure they have not been exposed to Pesticides, Insecticides, parasites or metal poisoning. If you do decide to use wild caught then Locusts, Grasshoppers, Katydids and Dragonflies are all good options. You can also use certain Moths but you need to research about their toxicity first.

A good rule when feeding is to always give proper sized prey that is suitable for the size of your chameleon. Prey should never be longer than the width of their head. This means smaller crickets will be needed for babies.

If you are feeding larger insects make sure they're soft bodied or have shed first as an insect with a large exoskeleton is often difficult to digest and may cause impaction.

Leaves

Whilst Jackson's Chameleons are insectivores some will enjoy eating vegetable matter although this is dependent upon the individual, whilst one may enjoy a few leafy greens now and then, another may just ignore them. It isn't too important if your chameleon does or doesn't eat plant matter as long as your insects are properly gut-loaded however, it is always a good idea to offer vegetables anyway. The best way to do this is to put it in a container with the feeder insects. If your chameleon eats it then great, if not your feeder insects will munch on it and the nutrients will then be passed on via them. Examples of fruit and vegetables to introduce to your Jackson's Chameleon include apple slices, leafy greens, bean sprouts and sugar snap pea pods.

I always think it's a great idea to wash any vegetable matter in warm water first before giving it to your chameleon. Not only does this ensure that they are free from harmful bacteria, insects or dirt that could become compacted in their gut, all of which can make them ill, but also because if they are slightly wet it may make them more tempting for your chameleon and gives them that extra drinking water.

Supplements

All captive chameleons need calcium and vitamin supplementation even when insects are gut-loaded. This is because these lizards need

Vitamin D3 so that they can metabolize calcium for growth. In the wild they would receive this from basking in the sun all day and this is another reason why natural sunlight is essential for your chameleon's health but as it isn't always possible for captive chameleons to receive the proper amount of natural sunlight supplementation is used instead.

Juveniles should have their food dusted daily with a calcium supplement containing Vitamin D3. For an adult this can be reduced to two to three times a week. Pregnant females should also have their food dusted more often as they will need additional calcium supplements during this time.

A reptile safe multivitamin which doesn't contain Vitamin A should be also be used 2-3 times a week. Although this is important for all species of chameleons you need to be especially vigilant with your Jackson's Chameleon as they are extra sensitive to excess amounts of synthetic Vitamin A and this has been linked to Gout and Edema. Use a multivitamin that contains Beta Carotene instead, as your chameleon can convert this into Vitamin A should it need to.

Avoid those supplements with added phosphorous unless specifically directed to by the vet as too much of this can cause Kidney Disease.

Some people recommend dusting your feeders in bee pollen as it is a good source of Protein, Enzymes and Amino Acids as well as Vitamin B, which is often used to stimulate appetites in anorexic animals. It is thought that bee pollen therefore can reduce the risk of your chameleon going on a 'hunger strike'. In the wild many insects will be covered in bee pollen before they are eaten by the chameleons so as long as you buy one that is safe for consumption then it can be a good, natural supplement to use. You can buy this either in powder form via the Internet or in tablet form from a health food store. These tablets can be easily ground up into a fine powder, which can then be dusted on your feeder insects.

Dusting means exactly that – a very light dusting. Don't smother your feeder insects in supplements, as if your chameleon gets too high a dose this can be dangerous to their health.

Although I have stated you should dust two to three times a week it should only be used as a guide as it is difficult to say exactly how much your Jackson's Chameleon should be supplemented because each one is different depending on their owner and set up. If your chameleon is going outside and getting a high level of natural sunlight and you are gut-loading your crickets and other insects thoroughly then they may need less Vitamin D3 and Calcium than one which never goes outside.

It is important that you don't over supplement so it is always recommended that you remain vigilant and talk to a vet in order to get advice that is tailored to you and your pet.

How To Feed

There are a variety of different ways to feed your chameleon. Some people will simply let the crickets or feeders loose in the cage for the chameleon to hunt; known as free ranging. This gives them activity and exercise and recreates more of a natural situation that they would encounter in the wild. However, some Jackson's Chameleons will not hunt for food or eat whilst somebody is watching them and crickets and other small creatures can easily escape unless you have cricket proofed your cage thoroughly. A smaller chameleon in a large cage may also struggle to hunt and find all of the prey you have let loose in the cage.

Another way to feed live insects is to put them in a plastic cup and securely hanging them or attaching them to a tree or branch inside the cage using twist ties. If you place some small pieces of fruit or vegetables into the cup as well then your feeder insects will continue to gut load whilst they're waiting to be eaten. This means your Jackson's Chameleon will still get the nutrients even if they don't actually eat the fruit or vegetables themselves. Make sure the cup is clean each time you feed and if you have more than one chameleon or lizard make sure you use different containers to feed each one to avoid potential cross contamination of bacteria or disease.

Keep the feeding cup low in the tree or on a branch near the bottom of the cage. This is because chameleons like to hunt their prey and will usually approach from an upward position as this helps them to avoid the top or side of the feeding container. Most chameleons can be easily trained to feed from a cup and may even come to expect food to be in there.

Some people will hand feed if their chameleon will let them and whilst this is good for bonding it shouldn't be done for every meal. You can also use tweezers or small tongs if you don't want to touch the insects.

How Often Should You Feed?
Neonates should be fed as many small crickets as they can eat several times a day.

Babies (3-6 months) should be given ten to twelve small crickets daily.

Juveniles (6-12 months) should be fed around 8-10 medium sized crickets daily. You need to be very careful not to overfeed and this life stage is the most difficult for a lot of chameleon owners. There is a high risk of developing Metabolic Bone Disease by overfeeding or misjudging the calcium to food ratios. Instead of offering a high volume of food, which can make it difficult to manage supplementation, offer food little and often so your chameleon can grow steadily and slowly.

Adult Chameleons (12 months and above) should be given 6-8 adult crickets every other day.

I've only put the food amounts in crickets here, as for most people this will be the main staple food that they feed the majority of the time. If you are providing a variety then just substitute this for crickets. For instance if you are feeding your adult Jackson's Chameleon a couple of mealworms one day then provide them with a couple less crickets. The best way to ensure your chameleon isn't overfed is by counting the amount of insects you feed and how many remain. For instance, if you feed your juvenile Jackson's Chameleon eight crickets and you find that you always have two remaining then you could reduce this to six crickets a day instead.

Make sure that any food that is uneaten is removed from the cage otherwise they can turn on your chameleon and bite them.

When To Feed
You should feed your Jackson's Chameleon in the morning, not long after their lights are turned on if possible. Feeding in the evenings or at night time - although it may be more convenient for you to watch them - isn't recommended because it can be unhealthy for your chameleon as they need the heat and activity they get during daylight hours in order to digest their food.

What To Avoid
There are lots of insects that are poisonous to chameleons. These include Ladybirds, Fireflies, Spiders (certain ones are poisonous but the best way is to avoid them all unless you are absolutely sure they're okay), Scorpions, Centipedes, hairy caterpillars and other poisonous insects as well as bees, wasps and anything that stings –

always check before you feed anything new to your chameleon. The list of what to feed and what to avoid is too vast to include everything here.

There are also foods to avoid when gut-loading because they are low in calcium and high in phosphorous, oxalates and/or goitrogens, these include cabbage, iceberg lettuce, spinach, broccoli, tomatoes, romaine lettuce, potatoes, corn, bread, cereal, grains and oats, beans, eggs, meat as well as dog or cat food and fish food.

You can buy canned crickets but they can also be high in phosphorous, oxalates and goitrogens and they don't have a high nutritional value; just like with human food, fresh is best.

Vertebrates such as lizards and pinkie mice are often on the list of things that chameleons eat and although they may indeed feed on these in the wild they wouldn't eat them in high volumes. Your Jackson's Chameleon isn't a carnivore and feeding them these creatures can wreak havoc on their kidneys leading to kidney failure and gout because they are unable to process the high amount of proteins found in these vertebrates. Everything your chameleon needs can be provided by properly gut loaded insects and correct supplementation.

A question many people will ask is "can I feed dead insects to my chameleon?" Live insects are preferable because, like water, moving insects will catch their attention whereas dead insects won't. If you have live insects that you are gut loading which suddenly die you shouldn't really feed these either unless you are certain of what caused their death, as they may have eaten something or be host to some sort of parasite that could make your chameleon ill.

Chapter 6: Settling In

As tempting as it may be, DON'T buy a Jackson's Chameleon on a whim. Don't ever say "I'm just going to look" if you know you have no willpower to say "no thank you, I'm just looking today"!

To be a responsible chameleon owner you need to have its new home set up in advance. You need to have had at least a few days checking the temperature and humidity levels and adjusting wherever necessary to ensure that these are correct for when your chameleon moves in, especially if you haven't had a lot of experience with keeping chameleons. Only when this set up is prepared and correct should you buy this type of lizard.

If you buy your chameleon from the Internet or mail order it will most likely arrive in a small box. Travelling will have been a frightening ordeal and the creature will need time to adjust to its new surroundings. If the box they arrive in is small enough to put in their cage do so and let your chameleon venture out when it's ready.

Although you will probably be dying to pick them up straight away or spend hours staring at them, resist the temptation and put their well-being first. These creatures don't like feeling as if they're being watched so if possible cover their cage with a thin blanket and leave them alone to get used to their new surroundings. It is important to make sure everyone else in the household does the same, including children. Keep any other pets away too and make sure the room they're in is kept as quiet as possible. Other than feeding and spot cleaning the cage you should ignore your chameleon altogether. As I said in the beginning, this may seem cruel but they aren't friendly animals like puppies, they need time to adjust and relax.

This should be the same process for any chameleon of any age, no matter where you bought it from. Remember if it came from a pet shop or a previous owner (even if you've bought it from a private seller with its cage and everything in it) its outside surroundings have still changed. It's still had to travel to get to you and it's now got to get used to new sights and smells.

After a couple of days you should be able to remove the cover although it's important that you continue to use this at night in order for your chameleon to get a good night's sleep.

During the acclimating process avoid rearranging, adding or removing any plants, rocks or 'furniture' in the cage. The territory is unfamiliar enough and any changes, no matter how small, will make it more difficult for your chameleon to settle.

A good way to get your new pet familiar with its new home is to put some live crickets loose in their cage. This will give them an activity as well as encouraging movement, which in turn helps them map out the layout of their cage. Use small (nymphs not adults) crickets that have been dusted and release them on the side walls or vines. Keep them climbing, as if they fall on the floor they will most likely die and won't garner much interest.

Don't worry if your chameleon doesn't eat for a few days when you first buy it. It is a normal reaction to a new environment. It will be assessing for threats and predators, most likely it will be wondering why you haven't eaten it yet! Once it feels settled then it will start to eat. If you release live crickets then cover the cage they may feel more comfortable to hunt knowing nobody is watching them.

New chameleons that are afraid to expose themselves may opt to hide in the middle or back of the cage throughout the day and may even avoid basking. Although this is normal it means their body temperature may not increase enough to enable good digestion, which will in turn have an effect on eating. If this is a concern you have then if possible, raise the overall room temperature but just ensure it's not so hot your chameleon overheats, whereas with a basking light your Jackson's Chameleon can leave that spot and move down the cage to a cooler temperature, if you have a hotter overall temperature it may affect the gradient temperatures of your cage. Remember Jackson's Chameleons like low heat and high humidity so you will need to check these regularly. Raising the overall room temperature should be a temporary solution too. Once your chameleon starts to feel secure they will begin to bask by themselves and you can adjust the room temperature again accordingly.

Once your chameleon stays in open view when the cover is removed, they are starting to settle. If they continue to stay out whenever you're near the cage rather than trying to hide as soon as you cast a shadow over their cage then you're already a third of the way to taming (see next chapter).

Chapter 7: Handling And Free Ranging

A lot of chameleon owners have stated that they can handle their chameleons without causing stress and indeed there are a number of videos and photographs that have been posted on the Internet of seemingly calm chameleons, of a variety of species, interacting with their owners, whether that be eating out of their hand, sitting on their heads or shoulders or being held gently on their lap being stroked. This is being held out as proof that chameleons can be tamed.

Whilst I'm not condemning people who do this as bad owners I would remind you here that chameleons are wild animals and there is far more evidence to suggest that they don't enjoy being handled than there is to the contrary so handling is not recommended. These animals are sensitive and my view is that they should be treated like exotic fish – observed but not touched.

Call me sceptical but I don't believe these creatures ever truly 'bond' with their owners, despite what some people say. There are those that state their chameleons come straight over and climb on their hand as soon as they open the cage door because they have a strong bond. Although I can't possibly say for certain how every chameleon in captivity feels, the negative part of me thinks that these chameleons simply associate their owner with food and know that by waiting at the cage door they are more likely to get insects, if their owners give them treats whenever they move to the door when they sense their presence then the chameleon may even realise that it's going to get something it enjoys.

Whilst I'm never going to believe that these chameleons love their owners in the same way a dog or a cat might, what these anecdotes do show, together with the aforementioned photographs on the Internet, is that it is possible in some cases to pick them up without causing too much undue harm or distress.

Time

This will take A LOT of work and time. You're not going to wake up one morning to find your chameleon running over to the door of its enclosure excited to see you. Nor is your baby chameleon going to jump out of its box and give you a great big hug as soon as you've purchased it. Instead it is a gradual bonding and understanding that will only come over time as your chameleon starts to see you as less of a threat.

It is suggested that you spend at least fifteen minutes a day to work on bonding. Try and choose the same time every day to develop a routine so your chameleon will know when to expect you.

Timing is also key - only try to handle your chameleon if it is near the front of its cage either climbing on the door or ceiling or if it's sat on a branch near the front. If your chameleon is hiding in the back or centre of the cage or is under its basking light then LEAVE IT ALONE. I cannot stress this enough. Reaching deep inside a chameleon's cage is along the same lines as trespassing and will only hinder your attempts to bond by stressing your chameleon out more and making it feel unsafe and insecure.

Temperament

Whether your Jackson's Chameleon reacts well to handling will depend on their temperament. Just like people, some are friendlier and more docile whilst others are grumpy and aggressive. You may simply end up with one who is in the latter group and will hate any contact despite how patient you are and how much time you invest in them. Unfortunately this is simply bad luck but I urge you to enjoy your chameleon from afar and love them anyway.

Even if you never touch them they are such fascinating creatures to watch and for a true chameleon lover just being able to observe them will bring endless joy. Please don't buy any chameleon with the sole purpose of being able to handle them and show them off on the Internet and to your friends.

A baby chameleon will get used to handling better than a juvenile although that isn't to say an older chameleon won't ever let you handle them, just that it may take a lot longer to establish that initial bond. How the chameleon has been treated by humans in the past will also affect their mood.

Small scale breeders will often handle and pamper their babies from the day they hatch so these chameleons will become used to handling. This is because most breeders know a lot of owners will want to be able to pick them up at some point and it is handy if ever you need to take them out of their cage to clean it, take them outside for natural sunlight or to take them to the vets for a medical. However wherever you buy a chameleon from you need to be aware that if it has been mistreated then naturally the chameleon will be wary.

Their journey to you will also have an effect on their personality. Most chameleons are put in dark boxes when travelling to or from pet shops or - if you purchased from the Internet – to get to you. If your chameleon's journey was traumatic it will take a long time for it to get used to its new surroundings and feel settled so you should always take this into account before even thinking about handling.

Also consider their housing situation before they came to live with you. If they were in a pet shop and have been kept in a cage with other chameleons they are bound to be stressed and highly strung. Whilst they may calm down in time, some may not.

How To Handle
The best way to start is with food in order to garner their interest and gain their trust.

If you have been cup feeding then the best way to do this is to hold the cup during feeding instead of hanging it on a tree. Your chameleon may back away or display signs of aggression the first few times you do this and if you see these signs you should always secure the cup in its usual place, shut the cage and leave them alone. You can keep trying each day until your chameleon eventually settles. This may take weeks, months or longer but you will need to persevere. Just always remember to back off immediately at the first sign of stress.

Once they seem fine with you holding the cup for them then the next stage is hand feeding. If you are trying to handle your chameleon then you should have had them long enough to know which snacks they enjoy. Place one of these either in the palm of your hand or between your fingers. The palm is often better because chameleons often mistake fingers as food. Open the cage VERY SLOWLY - another thing I can't emphasise enough. Whenever you handle your chameleon or are near its cage your movements need to be incredibly slow so as not to spook them.

Watch your chameleon very carefully. If they don't retreat then hold the prey around 20 cm (8 inches) from them – remember their tongue is super long!

Their eyes should be fixed on the prey not on you. If your Jackson's Chameleon sees the prey but then is more focused on you – think of that frightened, 'rabbit caught in headlights' type look – give up and try again later. Remember the objective here is to gain your chameleon's trust - it's a long term relationship you want to build not a temporary, forced one.

Make brief eye contact with your chameleon when you first open the cage but then turn your head away slightly so you can still see what they're doing but you're not staring. Never stare as this can be seen as threatening. No matter how much you love them your chameleon is initially going to see you as a predator and threat. Also sometimes these creatures don't like to eat if they think they're being watched. If your chameleon freezes with its tongue sticking out of its mouth then this is a sign that it's unsure and unwilling to eat with you watching.

Don't worry if your chameleon doesn't respond positively at first. It can take a very long time but stick to the same routine every day, trying to get a little closer each time but remembering to always pull away at the first sign of fear. The last thing you want is to cause your chameleon unnecessary stress. Eventually your chameleon should just snap food out of your hand.

A note of caution here – handfeeding should only be used as a way of taming and bonding *not* for primary feeding. You should only hand feed a few food items each day. The rest of your chameleon's food should be given in feeder cups or roaming free in the enclosure for your chameleon to hunt. Also remember that your chameleon needs time to digest it's food so if you are giving treats try not to do the taming routine too late in the day so that they still have a couple hours to bask.

Once they've started eating from your hand and seem confident and happy to do this, you could try putting some food on your arm to coax them to climb. Remember they will be nervous when they first do this so try not to move at all. It is very important that you stay close to the cage so that they know they can escape back to familiar territory whenever they want to. They tend to walk in a fairly straight path so may walk slowly up your arm. Extend your other arm to guide them back to the cage.

Whenever your chameleon is on your arm or hand you will need to try and keep your face at a distance and hold your chameleon slightly higher than eye level if possible.

Every time they climb onto your arm willingly don't forget to give them a treat to reinforce this behaviour.

Free Ranging
Once your chameleon is used to hand feeding without trying to run and hide you can try to 'Free Range' them. To do this tie one end of a bendy vine to one of the upper branches of the cage and the other end to a fake tree or climbable area a few feet away from the cage then very slowly open the door and hand feed to encourage them forward then step back, letting your chameleon find his own way out.

At first they may be reluctant to leave but eventually they should venture out although it may take a few attempts – don't expect them to come running out excitedly as soon as you open the door.

Once they seem comfortable, hand feed them but now of course you can get closer as they are out of the cage. Again, don't move too fast and no sudden jerky movements. You want your chameleon to show interest when you're offering the food by touching or smelling your finger. Flatten your hand and offer a worm (or whatever their favourite treat is) so that they have to climb onto your fingers. As mentioned earlier, chameleons don't like anything in their environment to change so when you're free ranging keep everything exactly the same. If they have a vine to climb, always make sure this is in the same position, develop a daily routine that is the same each time.

As your chameleon gets used to you try to gently touch their nose or head every day if they let you.

You may find that your Jackson's Chameleon won't go back into their cage by themselves after free ranging and this is the time when you will most likely be able to pick them up and handle them, especially if they've been without a heat source for a while.

To return them to their cage, flatten your hand directly in front of them. It is important that your chameleon can see this. Gently nudge your hand underneath the chameleon so that they grasp it, one foot at a time. Use your other hand to gently guide them forwards. Once on your hand, slowly return them to their home. Never put your chameleon close to your face as it may get scared and jump off which can lead to injury. Your chameleon may gape and get huffy but if you've managed to get them to this stage then they probably won't bite so don't panic. Move very slowly and calmly. Eventually you may be able to try and gently stroke their leg or chin with the tip of your finger.

Points To Remember
At the risk of repeating myself these are the important points to keep in mind when trying to bond and train your chameleon.

- Always move slowly and carefully – no sudden or fast movements.

- Never stare.

- Let your chameleon lead the way with your relationship. If they try to run, hide or show signs of stress or aggressive behaviour always leave them alone and try another time.

- Never push, corner, hover over or grab your chameleon – they will always see you as a predator if you do this.

- Always stay close to their cage so they can go back if they need to.

- Be patient – chameleons aren't like cats or dogs; they won't develop a relationship with you immediately. In fact realistically you may never actually bond although some chameleons may tolerate handling more than others.

- When feeding or holding your chameleon stay as still as possible.

- Respect their mood. Even after you've had them out a couple of times successfully there will always be days when your chameleon just won't want to be handled such as when they're basking, shedding, have just eaten or near bedtime.

- Always make sure the room is empty of other pets and people. Young children should never be around chameleons as they're too noisy and often too jumpy and unpredictable and they definitely should never be around them unsupervised.

- Try different foods.

- Follow the same routine at the same time every day.

Outdoors

No matter how great your chameleon set up is, a light bulb is no substitute for the long term benefits of real sun rays. Exposure to natural sunlight is even more important for those creatures, like the Jackson's Chameleon, that give birth to live so even just a few hours on a weekend will be beneficial.

There are three ways to get your chameleon outside; either by building an outdoor enclosure, carrying them outside in a cage, or free ranging them. There are advantages and disadvantages to each.

Outdoor Enclosure

Of course this is a great solution but you need to decide whether you would keep your chameleon outdoors all the time or just every now and again. Keeping them outdoors forever and never bringing them inside has its advantages – you could probably keep your insects outdoors too and there is no risk of any creepy crawlies escaping into your home should they manage to get out of the cage before they're eaten.

Depending on the climate you live in, you may not need heat lamps and all the equipment associated with those and because the chameleon will be getting real sunlight and absorbing D3 from this source you can reduce or possibly even get rid of some, if not all, of your calcium supplements.

No worrying about turning the lights out, they will be ruled by nature and day and night cycles will be natural.

Your cage can be as large as your garden allows, as chameleons are arboreal creature then tallness is key and theoretically it could be incredibly tall – after all there's no ceiling to take into consideration.

Whilst these may sound like the ideal set up realistically this isn't always do-able. For one thing you need to think about the environment that you live in. If you are in England where it rains a lot your chameleon is most likely to end up in a cage that is constantly wet. If you're in a hot country you may find that they are getting too much heat and sunlight and whilst this can be counteracted by misting more often and providing more plants to give them shelter from the sun, a Jackson's Chameleon will not thrive in a high heat.

Different climates would also mean humidity would be another factor to take into consideration and an outdoor enclosure, depending on what it's constructed of, may mean humidity levels drop or get too high.

Yes, it would be amazing to have an enclosure that is huge but how long will it take to clean it and is there a risk of insects hiding and not being eaten because your chameleon can't find them?

There's also the worry that your chameleon will be constantly stressed if you live in a noisy environment with neighbours' kids yelling or loud traffic noises. Add to this the risk that they may be eaten by the neighbourhood cat or a passing fox and outdoor living may not be all it's cracked up to be. However, now and then with you keeping a watchful eye on them may be a great way to give them natural sunlight.

Small Cage Carried Outdoors

I'm hoping your chameleon's cage is too tall to be transported about although some screen cages are incredibly light so it could be do-able. Temporarily you could house them somewhere smaller where they can sit outside and get sunlight or you could have a permanent outdoor cage that you put them in to get sunlight before bringing them back outdoors.

If you do have a temporary house to take your chameleon outdoors then of course this would need to have a mesh top or some sort of material that allows the sunlight through. You don't want them in an all glass enclosure where your chameleon will get cooked as soon as it's sat out in the sun. It still needs plants and branches in as well in order to allow them to escape the sunlight when they get too hot and preferably be tall so they can climb. Meeting all your chameleon's needs may not be doable in a small, transportable cage. Some people do take them outside like this but you may be hindering your chameleon's health rather than helping so it needs to be thought through carefully.

Outdoor Free-ranging

A lot of owners do this and it is successful. Your chameleon gets direct sunlight without a cage or screen filtering it first. This is perfect for increasing their Vitamin D3 levels plus they will get much needed exercise as they'll most likely explore the new area. You will need to make sure your garden has trees or bushes though because again, when they get hot they will need to shelter underneath in order to regulate their body temperatures. Also they won't want to be exposed to predators so foliage will make them feel secure.

Once you are able to handle your chameleon then it would be a great idea to carry them outside and place them on a low branch of a tree or on a bush. Using the same bush or tree each time means your chameleon will get used to being there and will settle easier.

A word of warning here though, if you do take your chameleon outside and they're not in an enclosure, keep an eye on them at all times. Whilst these creatures may mainly seem lumbering and slow, they can be quick and easy to lose. If you have a lot of foliage about they can become camouflaged or worse – without someone carefully watching over them, they can easily be carried off by a bird or other predator. I've heard so many stories about people who have put their chameleon on the lawn, run inside for a few minutes only to return and find their chameleon is no longer visible. It's a sad story but the moral is – don't leave your chameleon exposed outdoors. Of course, you may not have the time to just sit outdoors with them in which case, again, a cage is a safer option and free ranging should be left for a time when you are able to sit with them.

No matter which option you choose for exposing your Jackson's Chameleon to natural sunlight, always keep a close eye on them and look for signs of overheating. If they turn very light or begin panting or gaping you will need to move them to the shade as quickly as possible as these are signs of heat stress. If you spot any of these signs you should also give them a quick misting session in order to rehydrate them.

Tracking

There are lots of people out there saying "help, I've lost my chameleon!" Often it's in the cage and their enclosures are set up so perfectly they cannot find them because the chameleon is hiding away for a while after basking until its temperature has cooled back down. If you know it's inside its home, although it can be frustrating if you want to see them all the time, it's actually a good thing because it means your chameleon feels secure and you know it's safe.

However, sometimes people free range their chameleons outside without supervision and find their pet has disappeared completely. This can be devastating. They will run around in a panic, searching and worrying. Sometimes they find them, sadly often they don't. This leads to people asking whether it is possible to put a tracking device on a chameleon…

There are two types of tracker you can get for pets, one is micro-chipping where a small chip is injected into the animal's skin, if ever it gets lost it only needs to be taken to a vet who will scan it and check it against the database to find out who it belongs to. It works for bigger animals but for a chameleon? Sadly it's just not possible. These creatures are just too sensitive and fragile and the whole process of microchipping would be too traumatising. Even if we could get a chip into them, realistically, who is going to be taking a chameleon that's roaming in the bushes to the vet?

Often people won't recognise them, yes they may identify it as a lizard but if you live somewhere where creatures who look similar to chameleons live in the wild anyway, people won't always assume it's a beloved pet. Even if they did, how would they capture something that's aggressive and dislikes even its loving owner? Your chameleon isn't going to walk up to them and happily climb into a box – it's natural reaction will be to retreat into the bushes or else it will hiss and may even bite if they get close enough. Therefore microchipping isn't the answer.

The other types of tracking device for pets that are available on the market are small medallion type objects, about the size of a coin. When the animal goes missing you can locate it using your smartphone or similar device and it will ring audibly or display on a map using GPS signals so you can find it easily.

I see two problems with these devices with regards to chameleons – one is that even the tiniest of these objects are most likely going to be too big for it. I can't see it being very easy to attach it nor can I see this happening without causing stress.

The second problem is that GPS tracking, as great as it is, isn't always accurate so if your chameleon is just in a bush in your garden it may display a map of your area but I doubt it will pinpoint the exact bush or tree your chameleon is sat in. You still have the problem of finding it when it's camouflaged.

The bad news therefore is that there isn't a tracker available on the market at the moment for chameleons. Whether there will ever be one remains to be seen. A moneymaking idea for anyone that comes up with a suitable one! Part of me hopes there isn't, I think it may encourage people to become blasé towards these creatures, leaving them outside for longer periods. Remember it's not just the worry of your chameleon wandering off but the danger of it being carried away by a predator. The best way of keeping your chameleon safe is to just watch it at all times.

I can give you this piece of advice though - should you lose your chameleon outside look high up. Think about how these creatures will act in the wild. Arboreal creatures will always try to climb as this is a natural instinct and they also like the sun so look around for suitable spots that your lizard may have tried to climb in order to reach sunlight.

If you haven't found your chameleon by nightfall don't give up. Someone once gave me this helpful tip – get a torch and search in the garden when it gets dark. Sleeping chameleons are relatively easy to spot at night because their skin becomes paler, contrasting with the darker leaves of the shrubs. Therefore it is often easier to find them in the dark.

Chapter 8: Medical Problems

A lot of illnesses in these creatures can be avoided and the majority of medical problems arise because people buy a chameleon and don't understand their basic needs, their life in the wild or how to create the optimum environment. That's not to say that they will never get sick or that you're a bad owner if they do, just that if you keep your chameleon in an optimal environment, feed and water them correctly and understand about temperatures, heating and lighting, et cetera then you have a better chance at keeping your pet healthy for a longer period of time as some medical problems can be avoided.

Owners often don't recognise the signs or symptoms of illness and diagnosing is very difficult because chameleons are wild animals and as such they are very adept at hiding any medical issues as this would be seen as a weakness in the wild making them easy prey. As such, by the time your chameleon displays any symptoms they may in actual fact have been ill for a very long time.

Parasites
It is normal for any chameleon to carry a few parasites, even those that are captive bred. Most wild creatures do and it's unrealistic to think otherwise but if they are out of control it could lead to extra stress or illness. There are different types of parasites, many of which are invisible to the naked eye, so it is important to take your chameleon for a vet check once a year. This should include faecal tests to check for gastrointestinal parasites as testing and treatment can eliminate them before they become a problem. You can collect fresh faecal matter – both the whitish urate and the brownish excrement – in a plastic or glass container which should then be placed in a bag to prevent desiccation. Remember to wash your hands thoroughly afterward.

Cause – Can be contracted through food and through poor hygiene levels.

Symptoms – Symptoms include failure to grow, loss of appetite, lethargy, abnormal stools, sickness, visible signs of worms, weakness, dehydration, eyes closed and vomiting.

Prevention - Prevention is often better than cure because some parasites such as Protozoa are difficult to treat. To keep parasites at bay it is important to make sure your chameleon's cage is ventilated and that you maintain a high level of hygiene. You also need to do this with the insects you keep for food so as well as spot cleaning your chameleon's enclosure daily to ensure parasites can't breed you should also spot clean the insects' environment too. Although insects you buy can contain parasites, the risk is a lot lower so try to use these instead of feeding your chameleon wild insects or vegetation or even better, breed your own. Regular vet checks can also help to catch these parasites early before they cause serious illness.

Wild caught chameleons usually harbour parasites even when they're labelled parasite free, so this is another reason to buy captive bred animals.

Constipation/Digestion Problems
Cause – Chameleons will often consume other materials along with their food. Usually this will pass normally but occasionally it can cause a blockage. The wrong temperature and lack of hydration can also cause digestion problems or a female may suffer with this when she has eggs.

Symptoms – Hanging over a branch and straining with nothing coming out. This can cause a prolapse.

Prevention - You can minimise this by not using substrate, keeping an eye on temperature levels and making sure your chameleon is basking throughout the day. Keep a close eye on their diet and environment and make a note of everything you feed, everything they eat and record the temperature and humidity levels. Keep them well misted and hydrated. For females, ensure there is an adequate laying bin.

Kidney Failure and Gout
Causes - Gout is when an excess of uric acids is produced in the blood. This is often caused by long-term dehydration or certain vet prescribed antibiotics.

Symptoms - It is a very complicated disease which has many symptoms and many forms including excessive drinking, not eating, reduced mobility, swelling and pain when walking or climbing and extremely aggressive behaviour (especially when joints are touched).

Prevention - It is a common cause of death in pet chameleons because low level dehydration is easy to miss. That is why it's really important to have the appropriate humidity levels as well as an effective water drip system combined with misting, as this should keep your chameleon properly hydrated. If you suspect your chameleon has gout then take them straight to the vet.

Stress
Captive chameleons of any breed are all prone to stress.

Causes – Poor or too much lighting, too much traffic in the household, dramatic environment changes, loud noises, other animals (including those of its own species) seeing it's reflection, poor handling (or handling or any sort) and being sprayed with cold water to name but a few.

Symptoms - Dramatic or dark colour changes, smelly or watery faeces, abnormally aggressive, different body temperatures, rocking, flattening its body, loss of appetite and excessive hiding amongst foliage.

Prevention – Make sure that the environment is quiet as much as possible and try to put their enclosure in an area of the house where people won't be constantly walking around. Keep other pets as far away as possible and house other Jackson's Chameleons out of sight of each other. Don't put any mirrors in or near their cage so they don't ever see their reflection as they will mistake this for another chameleon. For wild caught animals make sure they are in a large environment with lots of hiding places that is as natural as possible.

Edema
This is an accumulation of excess fluids on the subcutaneous layer of the skin, which causes swelling.

Causes - There are many causes but the main ones are being fed crickets or other feeders coated in excess vitamins or being in an enclosure that is too humid.

Symptoms – It is characterised by swelling that resembles a goitre in chest, throat and neck. Even pets who have lived in the same enclosure for a long time can develop symptoms so it is important that you closely monitor your pet and look for anything unusual.

Prevention – Avoid feeding on food that is gut loaded with too many vitamins and over supplementing. Avoid products that contain high levels of protein. Although gut-loading and supplementation is good for them it needs to be done in moderation, if unsure consult a vet. Also maintain good humidity levels and check these on a regular basis.

Upper Respiratory Infections

These are common in chameleons in captivity and are infections in the respiratory tract or the lungs (known as Pneumonia). If caught early enough they can be handled successfully.

Causes – The main causes are environmental contamination, poor care and husbandry issues.

Symptoms – Gaped mouth, too much mucus, inflammation, wheezing or popping sounds, or bubbling around the mouth and nose.

Prevention – Check for air quality and proper temperature of the enclosure regularly. Do a daily spot clean removing any litter including uneaten food and ensure you have good drainage, as insect cultures and dirty water can increase the risk. Do a thorough clean at least once a month.

A tip to check for respiratory problems is to hold your chameleon close you your ear and listen. If you can hear creaking noises then it is suffering from a respiratory problem. Steamy showers or a warm mist humidifier can help with these problems but you will need to see a vet.

Calcium Deficiency

Calcium is used to flex muscles. If there isn't enough calcium present the animal with draw it from the calcium stored in its bones making them weak and prone to fractures.

Causes – This is caused by an insufficient lack of calcium and Vitamin A or too much phosphorous.

Symptoms – These include soft bones, soft jaw, lack of appetite, lethargy and deformities in the spine and legs.

Prevention – Coat feeders in the correct amount of calcium. Make sure they're lightly dusted – you should have a specific container used to dust feeders that is different to those used to gut-load and another one used to feed them to your chameleon. Gut-load feeders with healthy greens and fruits (for water) – remember whatever they eat is stored in their gut and will go into your chameleon when they eat the insects, hence the term 'gut-load'.

Vitamin A Deficiency
Vitamin A is readily available in nature and in the wild a chameleon absorbs this regularly as they will often eat insects and small lizards that contain this vitamin.

Causes - In captivity however, their diet consists primarily of insects that lack Vitamin A.

Symptoms – Swollen limbs, reduced growth rate, loss of appetite, skin abnormalities, swelling in the eyes, upper respiratory infections, liver enlargement and bone abnormalities.

Prevention – Provide your chameleon with the most nutritious diet by offering as wide a variety of insects as possible and research which ones are good for them. Gut-load insects with vitamin rich foods such as apple, cornmeal, carrots, legumes, sweet potatoes, oranges, etc… Coat feeders with multi-vitamin supplements containing vitamin A approximately two to three times a month.

Dehydration
This is a lack of drinking water.

Causes – Not providing enough water through misting or drippers or not having enough adequate surfaces to collect water can cause serious internal issues.

Symptoms – Orange or yellow urate (instead of white), sunken eyes (not round and bulbous), loss of appetite and weak skin that won't revert back to normal when pulled.

Prevention – Make sure there is sufficient foliage available as this will catch the water making it easier for your chameleon to drink or to get moisture by eating the leaves. Keep an eye out to see if your chameleon is drinking falling water either from the dripper or from misting sessions. Mist regularly at a minimum of twice a day, ideally at least four times. If you see any symptoms listed above consult your vet immediately as dehydration can point to a serious health problem and if you know you are providing enough drinking water than it can signal an underlying cause.

Stuck Shed

Chameleons, unlike some reptiles such as snakes, don't shed their skin all in one piece but instead shed in patches. When they're ready to shed you will usually notice that they've turned an overall dull colour and their eyelids may 'pop' making them look even more bug-eyed than usual. This usually happens every four to six weeks. It happens because the body grows a new layer of skin, which starts to separate from the old. A thin layer of fluid forms between, pushing the old layer of skin away from the body.

Causes – If the enclosure is too dry, fluid won't be able to form between the old and new layer of skin and the lizard can't shed it.

Symptoms – Usually you will see large pieces of shed skin stuck to the chameleon's body, often around the eyes, tail and head.

Prevention – DO NOT PEEL any skin that you see as this is not only dangerous but painful. If it is stuck to the chameleon it means it is not ready to come off yet. Your chameleon may seem itchy and grumpy so you can make it easier by spraying your chameleon with water and, if they allow it, gently massage its skin until it starts to peel off.

Stuck shed rarely happens in the wild because it is a more naturally humid environment that these creatures live in. If your conditions are optimal then you may not even notice that your chameleon has shed its skin because in ideal conditions shedding happens quicker and often they eat it afterwards.

To prevent stuck shed you need to make sure your enclosure has the correct humidity levels and that you are misting correctly and regularly. Check that the last spray of the day has completed dried before putting the lights out. If you find your enclosure is still wet at night you may need to start your final misting session earlier.

If retained shed is severe and you cannot get it off, even with the correct humidity levels and spraying you may need to see the vet.

Bodily Injuries

These include injuries, cuts and scrapes. It is important to treat any cuts and scrapes no matter how minor they look to prevent infections. Large lesions or serious injuries may need the vet to attend to them to prevent septic wounds.

Causes – These can be caused by regular play or something more serious such as a falling bulb or the enclosure being knocked over, your chameleon being dropped when handled or being attacked by another chameleon or other animal. This can also be caused by too much stress – if your chameleon has seen another of its kind, for example, it can cause itself injury during its display of aggression.

Symptoms – As these are physical they're fairly easily identified. Watch your pet closely to see if it's in pain. Periodically examine it for cuts or scrapes. If your chameleon has suffered a major injury they may have large lesions or a limp.

Prevention – Careful handling at all times. Leave their home undisturbed and avoid moving it, ensure that children and other animals are kept away so they don't knock the enclosure over. House only one chameleon to a cage, out of sight of others.

Mouth Issues
Causes – Poor nutrition or husbandry, overcrowded cage, poor temperature regulation, improper phosphorous levels, vitamin deficiency, insufficient calcium levels and scratches or wounds to the mouth.

Symptoms – Brownish yellow matter or stains surrounding the teeth and gums. Swelling of the lower jaw or dehydrated matter around the mouth. If left untreated it can cause loss of appetite.

Prevention – Provide your chameleon with the proper nutrition it requires. Watch carefully and make sure there is nothing in the enclosure that they can eat which will damage their mouth.

Tongue Problems
Causes – Mouth infection, vitamin deficiency, muscular problem or physical damage or injury.

Symptoms – Failure to remove tongue when feeding, swollen gular area, swelling of the tongue or inability to put tongue back in their mouth. If the latter happens it is important to ensure the tongue remains moist. Another, very serious symptom is the failure to use the tongue at all to feed.

Prevention – Provide a good nutritious diet of a variety of insects which have been gut loaded 18-24 hours before being fed to your chameleon and ensure your chameleon cannot injure or do any physical damage to its tongue in the cage.

Thermal Burns
Cause – The lamp is too close to a branch putting it within reach of the chameleon.

Symptoms – Light green patch of skin, with or without blisters, which then turns black leaving a raw area that is prone to infection.

Prevention – Place your basking light at least 30 centimetres (12 inches) away from your chameleon and make sure there are no branches or vines near the light. Remember your chameleon can (and will) climb the cage walls or ceilings, their aim is to get as close to the light as possible regardless of whether they get burnt or not. If you do notice any burns you need to seek treatment from a vet immediately as your chameleon will most likely need antibiotics. The vet will also give you a cream to soothe the exposed area and prevent infection.

Metabolic Bone Disease
This is probably the top cause of growth defects and deaths in these animals. It is a very slow and painful killer yet a lot of the time it can be prevented.

Causes –This is usually a dietary deficiency or lack of ultraviolet light.

Symptoms – Early signs include the softening of bones, swollen joints, clumsiness, rubbery jaw and bowed legs. Advanced signs include tremors, broken bones, general weakness, anorexia, difficulty projecting tongue and trouble climbing.

Prevention – Chameleons need at least 12 hours of UVB light daily in order to properly process calcium from food. Being outside in unfiltered sunlight is the best but indoor bulbs are sufficient. Regular vet visits are also needed so that any signs can be spotted early.

These are the main diseases that appear in Jackson's Chameleons in captivity. Although the majority of symptoms are listed for each case your chameleon may display others.

Unlike a dog, your pet chameleon isn't going to be able to whine or bark to alert you to pain or illness, therefore you need to give your chameleon a health check regularly and be attentive to warning signs. The following is a check list of what you should be looking for:

- Any bodily injuries
- Sunken eyes
- Respiration difficulties or infections
- Excess mucus
- Foaming at the mouth
- Visible signs of stress such as abnormally dark colours with no apparent reason
- Restlessness or roaming around the bottom of their cage
- Difficulty walking
- Limited or no climbing

Please don't try and play vet – if your chameleon shows any of the signs of illness that are listed here or elsewhere in the book you need to take them to a vet, preferably one who specialises in Jackson's Chameleons or at the very least reptiles in order to get professional advice and treatment.

Chapter 9: Breeding

Whilst Jackson's Chameleons can be bred relatively easily in captivity, keeping the neonates alive once they're born is very difficult and even the most experienced breeders often have a high mortality rate. Now that we have the Internet owners and breeders can (and do) share their experiences with keeping these creatures successfully, which allows those new to the chameleon world become more knowledgeable.

As there is clearly a demand for these creatures as pets, I absolutely agree that breeders are important because without them these type of chameleons will just continually be taken out of the wild and I hope that one day more breeders will appear on the market. However, that being said, I would never recommend you breed your Jackson's Chameleons unless you are an extremely experienced owner and have had extensive experience in breeding other types of chameleons.

One thing to keep in mind is that a pregnant female Jackson's Chameleon could give birth to anywhere between eight and thirty babies, another reason not to breed them on a whim.

Why Breed?
There is a difference between breeding to raise babies and breeding to sell. However, breeding is still breeding, no matter what your motives you will still end up with a lot of baby Jackson's Chameleons. These are the main reasons I think people choose to breed.

More Chameleons
If you've got this far into the book then you know that raising any type of chameleon isn't cheap or easy yet people still keep them. Why? Everyone will have their own reasons but my guess is that

there's just something special about these creatures. They are endlessly fascinating whether it be watching them hunt and eat or just observing their colours. It may just be pride that you've managed to raise them successfully. Whatever it is they can be strangely addictive and once you have one you may find you want more and more. You may start with a male then add a female to your collection then you may have fantasies of breeding them, keeping a few and selling the rest. However, whilst you may have enough love for twenty or thirty, do you have the resources? Whilst we will go into this in more detail later on, I will say that if your motivation to breed is because you want more chameleons then don't do it. Why can't you just add to your collection one chameleon at a time? Trust me, the cost of buying and setting up one chameleon a year is a lot less than setting up and raising thirty baby Jackson's Chameleons all at the same time for at least three months or longer. Concentrating on the husbandry of a few animals will also ensure that it is still fun and won't take all your waking hours to care for them. More chameleons doesn't necessarily mean more enjoyment, in fact the opposite is often the case.

Fun And Experience
If these are the only reasons you're doing it then you are not going to worry about getting your investment back, instead it's just another facet of your hobby. It is also the best way to ensure your Jackson's Chameleons are well looked after because you are more likely to prepare for breeding slowly and over time, investigating and researching how to do it properly and concentrating on just one clutch. If you truly love your chameleons then there is nothing more special and exciting than seeing one hatch for yourself. It is a truly amazing feeling. Those who breed for fun are actually going to be better breeders because they will be thinking about how to properly take care of the animals rather seeing their females as a money making machine and selling the offspring off too early in a desperate bid to make a profit. Of course you're going to have to sell off most,

if not all, of your babies, it's not realistic to think that you can raise thirty Jackson's Chameleons for the next ten years nor can you just release them into the wild (they would not survive!). Those that start off breeding for fun with the intention of just raising one or two clutches often turn it into a successful side-line because they can show their superior husbandry which is often their selling point. Eventually they make a reputation for themselves and everyone wants to buy from them. This often leads to people placing orders, which means the breeder has often sold most of the creatures in advance, before they're even born.

To Save The Wild Chameleons
As I previously mentioned there is a market out there where people are capturing wild Jackson's Chameleons and selling them to people who are desperate for these pets. Many people, myself included, don't agree with this practice as evidence has shown that wild caught chameleons don't do well in captivity. This has led some people to believe that they should breed their Jackson's Chameleons because there is a market for them. You only have to do a quick Google search to realise that actually there aren't many breeders of this type of chameleon out there.

Whilst this is true, I don't think that regular owners should start to breed. Yes you may have kept a juvenile Jackson's Chameleon alive until the age of three or four and they may in fact be thriving but that doesn't mean you would have the ability to raise thirty babies successfully. One or two people breeding these creatures won't stop the black market of selling wild caught chameleons

Attention And Status
In some circles being a chameleon breeder is a status symbol. You hear breeders being talked about as if they are the experts on all things related to these lizards and in some ways this might be the case. However in order to be this great revered fountain of

knowledge you need to have that experience and that means raising these creatures successfully first as an owner, then as a breeder so you need to know what you're doing.

Maybe you want the attention that could be garnered from posting pictures on the Internet or making videos on YouTube of yourself surrounded by thirty baby Jackson's Chameleons?

If you are looking to breed purely as a status symbol or to establish yourself as an expert in the chameleon community I would try to dissuade you. You can make your ideas heard and give advice on a number of platforms without churning out a high number of chameleons. Not to put down the breeders that are out there but to get two a female Jackson's Chameleon to breed and give birth to ten or twenty babies doesn't necessarily mean you *are* an expert it just means that you've put two chameleons of the same species together. Keeping these babies alive is another story altogether and unless you know what you're doing I think it's just cruel to bring these babies into the world only for them to die.

Money
Okay I have to add it in here, we will discuss it further down as well but of course money is going to be the main reason for a lot of people to breed. It should really have been top of the list. Who doesn't want to make money doing something they love? However, it's not as easy as breeding two chameleons and selling the babies via the Internet. I'm not saying this can't be done but there are all sorts of factors that need to be taken into consideration.

Are you going to just mate your female once or twice to enhance your hobby and see what breeding is all about, with the money aspect just being a nice bonus or are you going to set up as a serious business? If it's a hobby then it could be relatively easy as you do what you've been doing and hopefully you will have contacts in the chameleon community and then just sell to those people. As you only want to make money to support your hobby you won't be panicking about selling them but rather planning and advertising your clutch in advance and of course having a back-up plan in case your chameleons are still with you when they hit the three to four month stage and need to be separated. Just remember that if you love your female chameleon dearly that her life span will be significantly reduced by mating and giving birth.

If you're breeding purely to make money and start a new business then you need to research and be certain that you can sell the babies once they're old enough to go to new homes. What you don't want to do is for your Jackson's Chameleon to give birth to twenty babies which you can't sell other than for a really cheap price. This won't make you money (or at least not a decent amount) nor will it do any good for the Jackson's Chameleons themselves as you risk selling them as cheap pets to people who will balk at finding out that a creature they paid £60 for costs £1000 or more to feed and house.

The Breeding Process
Okay so you want to breed, maybe for one of the reasons named above, maybe for your own reason but remember one thing - only healthy animals should be bred.

Choosing Your Chameleons
If you are buying a pair to mate then it is advisable that you buy a juvenile pair and raise them until they're adults before breeding. This is because if you buy two adults to breed (or you have one adult already and buy another) you can never be sure how old the adult that you purchased is and you may find that they're already too old to breed.

Once you have chosen your chameleons, make sure they are fully grown adults because although Jackson's Chameleons can reach sexual maturity at five to seven months of age, females are more likely to have reproductive issues if bred before twelve months so it is worth waiting. As with everything else related to chameleons, patience is a virtue.

There isn't enough scientific evidence that says inbreeding affects the general health of Jackson's Chameleons. When they were accidentally introduced in Hawaii in 1972, clearly there must have been some inbreeding in the wild for the population explosion we now see there today so it doesn't appear to have been a problem. Some breeders therefore will use this as an excuse to inbreed their Jackson's Chameleons.

However, not enough research has been done on the health of those chameleons and nobody can be really sure about how long they live in the wild and for that reason I would always recommend you start with a pair that are unrelated.

Breeding
Of course you are going to have to put a pair of Jackson's Chameleons together in order to mate but until you are ready to do so you should always keep them in separate cages and out of sight from each other, only putting them together for a short time in order for the breeding process to take place. If your male Jackson's Chameleon can see your female Jackson's Chameleon on a daily basis they may become familiar with each other and it may make them less inclined to mate when they are put in the same cage.

For your Jackson's Chameleons to breed the environment needs to be optimal and suitable day and night temperatures should be maintained year round to imitate the natural stimuli found in the wild.

When you think your two chameleons are ready to mate place them into the same cage. The theory is that if you place a female into a male's territory he'll be more aggressive and therefore breed with her in order to establish dominance. Some owners however do place the male into the females cage, as they find that it is less stressful for the female making her more receptive to mating.

Whichever way you do it, it is important that as soon as you introduce them you closely monitor the female over the next several seconds and focus on her reaction to the male. A female who is ready to mate will have a solid colouration from bright green to brown or greyish tones. An unreceptive female will have greys and black tones mixed in with the green. Watch for signs that your female is uninterested; this can be signalled by rocking back and forth, hissing or biting. If you see any of these signs then she isn't ready and you need to remove her immediately and try again a week or so later, otherwise she could get injured.

A male will try to woo the female by changing colours and swaying gently as if they are dancing. If the female is receptive she will change colour and mating will take place soon after. Around fifteen minutes later the male will either leave by his own accord or the female will make him leave by changing colour. Whilst you can mate your chameleons over the course of a few days you should monitor them closely and once they have been bred they should be separated otherwise the male will try to establish dominance which will be stressful for both of them.

Unlike some chameleons that lay hard shelled, fertilised eggs into the soil, Jackson's Chameleons' babies are grown in soft shell membranes inside the mother. Once the female has these eggs inside her she will start to expose them to the sunlight for a period of time each day so you need to ensure you have at least one suitable basking spot and (if your female is kept indoors) try to get your

Jackson's Chameleon outside into natural sunlight wherever possible. The gestation period can be anywhere between five months and nine months depending on the temperatures. Whilst you should give your pregnant chameleon more food and water during this time you may notice that eventually your female stops eating and drinking and this could be a sign that she's ready to give birth.

When she is ready your female Jackson's Chameleon will push her babies out as she's going about her day, pushing them out onto the branches and the floor. They are born in a soft sticky sac and they will be asleep until their mother deposits them on a branch. They will then wake and break out of the egg whilst the mother moves on to deposit the next one.

They should usually tear themselves free from the birth sac within about ten minutes. Humidity levels are incredibly important at this point because if there is low humidity in the cage the sacs may dry up quickly and the babies may struggle to free themselves. If this happens you may need to assist them. If humidity temperatures are suitable then only the weakest babies may fail to free themselves from the sac. Whilst you can help them, be aware that these may die regardless.

Hatchlings
Once the babies have hatched you should remove the young immediately. Whilst you may feel that the mother should be with them after they've just been born, they are at risk of being eaten, as the female Jackson's Chameleon will see them as moving prey.

The babies can be kept together until around three months of age when they have to be separated. However it is important that the smaller babies aren't bullied by the stronger, larger ones, which means you should monitor them all very closely. One way to ensure all the babies get their fair share of food and water without having to

100

fight for it is to separate them into different groups with like sized neonates being housed together. You will still have to monitor them though because they may grow at different rates so those that grow quicker will need to be moved into another cage with like sized cage mates.

Neonates may start eating hours after giving birth or days after. You can stimulate them to eat by lightly misting several times a day with lukewarm water; this will also prevent them from becoming dehydrated.

Baby Jackson's Chameleons are more adversely affected by very low temperatures than the adults so nighttime lows should be above 20 degrees Celsius (68 degrees Fahrenheit) for the first few weeks after being born.

The Female After Birth
Once she has given birth and the babies have been removed your female should be misted to ensure she can rehydrate. You should also offer her food in case she's hungry but don't put too much in her cage in one go. If she just wants to rest she won't want to be annoyed by crickets jumping around her enclosure.

Be aware that your female chameleon has the ability to store sperm so she could give birth three months after the first brood despite not having been bred again. Tests carried out on females that have died have shown them carrying three different generations all at the same time. If the sperm count is not high enough to fertilise all the eggs the female will produce only yolks so if you do want her to have another healthy brood you should reintroduce her to the male two weeks after giving birth, assuming she is in good health.

Factors To Consider

If you do decide to breed these animals it is important to identify what your motives are. There are many factors to consider which means it isn't as easy as just putting two of the same species together and waiting for them to mate.

Space – Okay so you have a spare room and in one corner is a tall, spacious vivarium housing a male Jackson's Chameleon. In the opposite corner, out of sight of the male is another tall, spacious cage with a female Jackson's Chameleon. One day you put your female in with the male and now she's given birth to twenty babies. Where do you put them? Maybe you've separated them by size and have put them into four separate cages, five to a cage. Do you have room for these extra five cages? What happens if thirty babies had been born, you could need seven extra cages if not more?

You sell maybe one or two, possibly five and ship them off when they reach three months…you still have over fifteen babies left. These creatures are now becoming more aggressive and territorial so you need to re-house them all separately. Do you have room for fifteen enclosures, all of which have to be a fairly reasonable size? Uh-oh, your female gives birth three months later, despite not having been mated again and has another ten babies, once again needing cages to live in, do you have enough room?

The reality is you may sell your baby chameleons but chances are you won't sell them all within three months when they need to be separated. You are going to need a whole lot of money and a whole lot of space.

Time – If you are a full-time breeder then that's great. You don't have to work to pay for this hobby as you are making enough money that your job is simply to raise these wonderful creatures. Lucky you! Not everyone is this lucky and for a novice breeder it would be worth remembering that if you have a job that requires you to work outside the house (even if you work from home) it's a pretty big commitment. Sure, whilst your female is pregnant you don't have to do much extra other than feeding and misting her more but you will need to be around when she's due to give birth otherwise she may eat the live young before you even realise she's had them. Once they've been born you need to feed them as much as they can eat. You need to mist them, preferably by hand to ensure their lungs don't become clogged with water. You are going to need to check the temperature and humidity levels at least once a day if not more on each enclosure. This can take a lot of extra time even if you only have a few to look after.

Each time you do these tasks you are going to need to record it all in a book to prove to buyers that your chameleons have been looked after. That means monitoring each one carefully. You are going to need to advertise your little critters so that you can sell them. You need to make up a care sheet and print these out to distribute to your new customers so that you are certain they know how to take care of them properly. You are going to need to clean each of the cages daily. The insects you gut-load are going to increase in number so you need to clean their tubs out as well and feed them, all on a daily basis. You may need to speak on the telephone to potential new owners. Don't forget you also have two adult chameleons to take care of. Do you have the time for all of this?

Let's say you do – what if you want to go on holiday? Who will look after all these baby chameleons plus two adults for you?

Cost – Yes I have the time. Yes I have the space... That's great. Can I just ask, have you recently won the lottery? Do you know how much baby chameleons cost to raise?

You have the cages – let's say twenty babies hatched and you house five together, that's four enclosures you need which can be around £160 (Around $216) each. That's £640 (around $864) in total. That's just the enclosure price. Yes, you can mist with a hand held spray bottle but baby Jackson's Chameleons, like adults, still need all the lighting and heating equipment. That's another few hundred pounds/dollars right there.

Then there is the food. Babies are constantly hungry and will eat huge amounts. Unless you have colonies of insects – mainly pinhead crickets and fruit flies for babies - that you breed yourself then you are going to spend a good few hundred pounds (or dollars) a month just on food. If you're going to seriously breed Jackson's Chameleons then I would suggest you do have your own insect farms but of course you have to gut-load and dust which increases your food and supplement bill.

Whilst many Jackson's Chameleons die very young for reasons that are unknown, many out there are being sold too young to inexperienced people who don't understand these creatures because breeders have realised far too late that they can't afford to feed so many mouths.

A Jackson's Chameleon may make you money, after all, there aren't many breeders around, however the cost of breeding and raising needs to be factored in. The hard truth is that although some breeders do make money, the majority of them lose it. It is an expensive hobby with just one chameleon never mind a whole army of them!

Not only that we haven't even covered vets bills or shipping costs…

As I mentioned earlier there is a difference between breeding and raising chameleons and making money. If your end goal is to make money then I would dissuade you from doing so immediately. Read the whole section above and then consider this – let's say for an example that you've spent £1000 ($1317) on cages, heating, lighting and a three months' worth of food and supplements. In the real world this cost is probably a lot higher, after all we haven't factored in increased water or electricity bills or your time. Not only that but are you really going to sell twenty chameleons locally or to people who are willing to collect from your home? If not you will have to factor in shipping costs, preferably using a company who is reputable and experienced in shipping these types of animals safely…again, that will significantly reduce the amount of money you make.

Are you really going to be lucky enough to sell every one of your Jackson's Chameleons at the three months mark? If not they are costing you money each month you keep them. Chances are if you are new to breeding and don't have a reputation yet, you will struggle.

If you do manage to sell them all off by three months then you may be lucky enough to make a small profit but is it worth it all the time and the effort? If you were breeding just to extend your hobby then yes, the money is a bonus but if you are doing it purely to make money then I don't think it's viable.

My intention isn't to put anyone off breeding, I am merely warning you and asking you think carefully… a lot of would be breeders find out too late that breeding isn't the get rich quick scheme they had imagined when they first started.

Where To Sell

If I haven't put you off breeding (or maybe you are a chameleon owner that has already mated your animals), you may be wondering how and where you can sell the offspring. In this day and age you are lucky because thanks to technology it is easier to connect with people and find those who want to buy a Jackson's Chameleon whether that is through an intermediary or direct to customers themselves.

As I've said before, don't sell before three months because this marks an age where the baby is big enough to handle being transferred to a new home and will have established a good track record of eating and drinking. This is important to keep as proof that your chameleons are healthy and well cared for.

So who do you sell them to?

Wholesalers
For breeders who want to make money, landing a wholesaler is the dream as they will buy in bulk and in turn sell them to various retail outlets. This means they would most likely buy all your babies from you and if you build up a good relationship with them, theoretically you could in fact sell every single Jackson's Chameleon your female ever gives birth to in one quick and easy step.

Before you say "quick sign me up", remember that you may not make a huge profit, usually a wholesaler will negotiate a deal that could be twenty five percent of the retail price so if this is £199, they could realistically pay £49.75 for each chameleon. For twenty therefore you would get £995 for thirty you would get £1492.50. Whilst this may sound a lot, if you've spent £1000 on enclosures, heating, lighting, food and increased water bills you aren't making that much profit (if any at all).

To make serious money with a wholesaler you would need to continually breed your female so that she gave birth every few months, which of course reduces her life span considerably. If you have a few females it may be easier and put less strain on each but none of your females will have long lives and they become more of an investment rather than a pet and you are putting money before the wellbeing of your chameleons.

Another disadvantage is, of course, you don't know who is going to get your baby chameleons – are they going to be sold to responsible owners or to pet shops who keep them altogether in a cage long after they should be separated then sold to people who buy them on a whim and then can't take care of them? Do you even care? If the answer to this last question is no, then I urge you not to breed at all!

If this is a route you want to take you can often find wholesalers advertising in the back of trade magazines or on the Internet, usually attached to sites dedicated to reptiles and even specifically chameleons. Usually their adverts will state that they don't sell to the public. Some may also be asking for whole clutches of captive bred chameleons, as they know these are better than wild caught.

Retail Outlets
Unlike wholesalers who sell to outlets, a retail outlet is the business that sells to the general public such as pet stores or sales websites. The upside of selling direct to these retailers is that you can negotiate a higher profit, sometimes 50% of the retail price. That means if they are going to sell for £199, you can ask for £99.50 for each chameleon. If you have twenty that gives you £1990 back, assuming you sell all of them.

The other advantage is that you can get an idea of who the end buyer will be and how your chameleons will be treated, if you sell to a pet shop who you know has one or two fish tanks in which they keep all their chameleons with a bowl of water in the corner, then you can bet that your babies won't have a long or happy life. If you sell to those who specialise in exotic pets however it is often fair to assume that they will give good advice to the end buyer and your Jackson's Chameleons will be cared for and go to good homes.

The downside is that retail outlets probably won't have the space to buy too many in one go therefore you may have to approach a few in order to sell all your babies.

To find respectable retail outlets search the Internet or the back of trade magazines or look for them at reptile shows. A lot of knowing who to sell to is down to experience but as a new breeder you won't have this so try and go for those who have a good reputation. Post on forums and ask for advice from the reptile or chameleon community.

Direct Selling
This is where the serious money is coming from, right? You're going to sell your Jackson's Chameleon for £199 minimum and everyone is going to come direct to you. Yes, this is kind of the idea, you've cut out the middle men so now you can sell for a higher price and you get to see what kind of homes your babies are going to and you can pass on your own expert advice so know that the new owners are going to be able to take care of them properly, plus you get to meet new people in the Jackson's Chameleon community.

However, the disadvantages are not everyone is going to buy from you and you are going to have to make multiple points of sales in order to get rid of all your babies. If you have twenty chameleons then you will need twenty customers. Not only that but you will also have to deal with the members of the public which means you are going to meet people who might be disagreeable and trying to take advantage of you by negotiating lower prices. You also have the added complication of shipping the chameleons as well as the risk of losing money and gaining a bad reputation should they not arrive alive at the buyers' end.

If you are letting people come to your house then you need to be prepared for anyone and any questions they may have. This means your husbandry has to be pretty perfect – the last thing you want is someone coming in who knows more about your chameleons than you, a breeder, does. Secondly, do you really want a bunch of strangers coming into your home? Some of them might be great but you also have to expect people who are just coming to nosy at your set up and ask questions without purchasing. This can be avoided by meeting in a public place, taking photographs of the set up and the babies with you although some people may want to see the chameleons in person.

One thing is certain, if you are selling direct you are going to have to advertise whether this be in trade magazines or via the Internet – setting up a website or selling via social media pages. It may be worth looking into selling at trade shows too. Whilst there is less competition amongst Jackson's Chameleon breeders compared to that of other breeds of chameleons, you are still going to need to build a reputation for yourself.

Unless you are lucky enough to live in a large city where people are willing to collect from you direct, you are going to need to become familiar with shipping and the shipping process which once again, means eating into any money you may make.

Breeders
If money isn't the reason you are breeding then you may be able to negotiate with other breeders to take your offspring to add extra blood lines to their breeding projects. Be aware that they probably won't pay a high amount as, like you, they probably aren't making a lot of (if any) money from this venture but purely doing it because it's a hobby they love. They may trade some of their own creatures for yours. You can search the Internet to find reputable breeders but try and do this in advance, as it will take time not only to find them but also to sort the good from the bad and build up solid relationships.

How To Be A Responsible Breeder

You need to ensure your chameleons are being kept in proper conditions. If you are breeding please make sure you –

- Only breed the healthiest animals.

- Raise babies in a way that gives them a good start in life.

- Don't sell any that you breed until it is old enough to be re-homed.

- Provide new owners with a care sheet and ensure they understand how to provide care.

- Check those buying from you have a suitable set up in advance.

- Discourage buyers who want two chameleons for breeding purposes from buying a pair that are siblings.

- Be open and honest and encourage buyers to come back to you with questions and provide them with the correct advice even after they've made a purchase.

If you are breeding because you love these animals and not to make quick, easy money then you should be willing to provide advice even if you know a customer may have bought a Jackson's Chameleon elsewhere. Although I don't agree that a novice should breed these creatures, I do understand that breeding is a necessity because obviously there is a market for them and if nobody bred them then it would only lead to more being taken from the wild which is cruel and irresponsible but because of how fragile these creatures are I would encourage anyone considering breeding to do this correctly and put the animals well-being before money.

Chapter 10: Common Myths

Chameleons, despite having been kept in captivity as pets for so many years, are still greatly misunderstood. There is so much information out there that is misleading and contradictory that it's impossible to know who to believe and who to ignore. What I have noticed through both experience and research is that there are some common myths which can lead owners, especially new ones who have no other experience to compare with, to thinking they are doing the right thing yet actually damaging these delicate creatures and doing more harm than good.

The common myths that you should ignore are –

Chameleons' Absorb Water Through Skin
This frustrates me no end. People will look at a chameleon, even in a photograph and say "oh its eyes are sunken, it's dehydrated; you should put it in a bath". The owner says something along the lines of "I've never heard of bathing a chameleon before" but then instead of ignoring this advice like they may have done fifteen years or so ago, they switch on their laptop, type 'chameleon bath' into the Internet search engine and are greeted with cute little pictures of chameleons in bowls of water.

What they ignore (or don't see) are the stress signals the poor creature is displaying. Chameleons DO NOT like bathing. You won't go in the wild and see them rolling about in puddles of water, their tongues lolling out of their mouths like puppies! They have evolved to live in trees. They do not sit in puddles of water splashing about nor do they drink from them. Although people will say spray your chameleon directly when misting, this is just to help keep their skin moist so they can shed easier, it has nothing to do with hydration as they do not absorb water through their skin, it is a myth.

I would also like to point out that yes, sunken eyes are a sign of dehydration but they can also point to other problems too. Stress, illness, parasites, infection and extreme weight loss can all cause eyes to become sunken. Rather than putting your chameleon in a bath to soak them, check your humidity and temperature levels and look at your misting techniques and the suitability of the enclosure itself. If you are certain your husbandry techniques are the best they can be then taking your pet to a vet that specializes in exotic animals for a faecal test and examination is the solution rather than a bath.

Glass And Substrate Kills
Hopefully I haven't been guilty of perpetuating this myth earlier in this book when I spoke about caging and substrate. Both of these are controversial topics, especially the latter and although I am not a fan of novice owners using them I don't want people to go off and start lecturing others for doing so. The myth that "glass and substrate will kill your chameleon" is another popular one.

When owners talk about glass enclosures being suitable they're not talking about a fish tank being placed on its end and having the top covered in screen but actual glass enclosures with a mesh or screen lid and vents at the bottom to allow air to circulate that have been designed especially for chameleons. The two are very different – a glass fish tank most likely will kill your chameleon eventually and I believe this could be where this myth began. The screen and mesh screens are most often recommended as they have the benefits of great air circulation as well as being lightweight and relatively cheap but chameleon owners have complained that it is difficult to maintain proper humidity levels because the airflow is so good and keepers then overcompensate by misting more regularly which makes the environment wet. A glass enclosure made specifically for chameleons however will help keep humidity levels high.

The problem is that there are people all over the world living in different environmental conditions – what is suitable in the UK where the air tends to be dry and cool may not be suitable for someone living in a naturally humid environment. You need to determine what type of environment you live in to find out which cage is suitable to you as an owner. If you just don't know I'd advise going on a forum and asking what other people in a similar area are doing – of course make sure these are experienced keepers who have raised a Jackson's Chameleon to at least five years if not longer rather than a new owner who has only had their chameleon a few months and are just quoting something they've found on the Internet.

Whatever cage you choose you need to check humidity and temperature levels daily and record them – not doing so is what kills chameleons, not the enclosures themselves.

And substrate? Yes it can cause impaction and I don't recommend it for novice owners but there's no denying it makes for a more natural environment. The key to avoiding impaction is keeping the chameleon in the correct environment with optimum temperature and humidity levels and a healthy diet consisting of a variety of insects and the correct amount of supplementation. That way even if your chameleon does swallow a tiny bit of soil it shouldn't cause impaction if your chameleon is healthy.

Chameleons Get Lonely

People stare into a chameleon's cage and think how sad they look. "You should get it a friend" they often remark. Hmm...possibly this is helpful advice for a rabbit or a hamster or whatever likes to be around other creatures. Is it the answer for my chameleon that loves his privacy? No. What people don't comprehend is that even in the wild these creatures will avoid each other. The difference is, in a wild environment they have all the space in the world to escape from one another. Each will have their own territory and they will stay separate, other than to mate. They like it this way, their lives are less stressful and that is why they live longer. As humans, we project our own feelings onto our pets, whether this is loneliness or something else. The truth is that chameleons are solitary creatures, they don't even like their own reflection and they definitely won't thank you for providing them with a friend. Instead, what people fail to see are the stress signals or aggressive displays such as the pacing around at the bottom of the cage, the changes in colours (they might be pretty but they also become brighter for a reason), the gaping and hissing, closed eyes, weight loss or even running away and hiding. If you put two chameleons together they will fight it out with the stronger and bigger one dominating the other. You may think they've calmed down and are happy but actually they are probably just tolerating the situation because they have no choice. In reality one will have dominated the other and both their lives will have been unnecessarily shortened because they are living in a state of heightened stress. Don't be fooled by the pictures that are being posted on the Internet of chameleons co-habiting or even having their cages next to each other – they may look sweet but the reality is very different.

Chameleons Love Their Owners
I'm shaking my head at this point because I'm so frustrated when I see photographs of people on the Internet with their chameleons on their shoulders or wrapped in blankets being carried out and about in public places, people fawning all over them. Not only is it perpetuating a myth but it's also cruelty in my book. Again, it's humans projecting our feelings onto these creatures. I don't want to sound mean but your chameleon isn't going to love you. It may climb onto your hand if you've got food – this is because you have food or it expects food! It may climb up your arm and it may allow you to hold it. This is tolerance not love. Do they enjoy it? I want to say no but some may like it, we can't be certain. What we do know is that they are wild animals, solitary in nature and prone to stress, you decide. Again, don't be fooled, a picture may paint a thousand

words but in the case of a chameleon these words have been very badly misinterpreted.

I'm not saying don't ever handle your chameleon but do so in moderation. Remember their enclosure is a micro-climate ideal to them, when you take them out of it you are subjecting them to alien conditions which will take a toll on their bodies. They can handle being removed at times for short periods but remember they need the correct light, humidity and heat to thrive and they don't get this sitting on your shoulder watching TV.

Give Food And Supplements In High Amounts
Yes your chameleon needs food.
Yes your chameleon needs supplementing.
However, the myth that you are going to have to feed your chameleon as much as it can possibly eat will shorten their life span. Baby chameleons need to be given as much food as they will eat – this is because they are growing and all the energy they receive from their food will be used for these growth spurts. Adult chameleons however, will have a slower growth rate so feeding them what they like will only cause them to put on weight. Your chameleon may well eat everything you give them but you need to be the responsible one who monitors their food levels. Remember in the wild they may eat a large amount one day but then not find any insects for a day or two. You make the feeding schedule based on their needs and ensure they are fed a healthy diet with a variety of insects.

If you gut-load correctly, provide a mixture of different creepy crawlies and take your Jackson's Chameleon out into the natural sunlight every now and then you may need very little supplementation. When you do supplement you need to lightly dust not coat your insects so that they are pure white. Too much supplementation is dangerous to the health of your chameleon. The chameleons who have longer life spans in captivity tend to be the ones who have very little supplements at all. With these creatures it is all about moderation and care, it is so complicated that if you are unsure you should check with a vet who is experienced in exotic animals, preferably with specific knowledge about chameleons.

Enclosures Need To Be Placed Near A Window
You've heard that Jackson's Chameleons need natural sunlight so of course why not put your cage near a window? It will also cause your plants to grow, right? Well if the mid-morning sun shines through the glass window the cage will act like a heat trap and basically your chameleon will cook. UVB rays don't penetrate glass either so it is a redundant act. Your chameleon needs natural, unfiltered sunlight, which means taking them outdoors and free ranging them. In winter, cold air falling from the window onto the cage will put your chameleon at risk of a respiratory infection or will cool them so much their metabolism slows down, making it difficult for them to digest their food and creating a whole host of problems. Put your enclosure in a corner away from direct sunlight and take them outside if you want them to have natural light.

Increase Airflow By Putting Enclosure Next To A Fan
Another no, no I'm afraid. You need to create a natural environment which means ventilation should be passive rather than forced. A fan or vent will force airflow into the cage; if you have one blowing through it all this will do is dry out the habitat, push away any humidity and eventually causes dehydration.

Misting And High Humidity Is Needed
Yes they do need this but they don't need to be constantly wet. Too much moisture caused by over-misting is often the first thing that kills chameleons in captivity. You need to hydrate your chameleon and regular misting sessions are a must but there needs to be a balance between the two. Think how the chameleon lives in the wild – it rains and this rainfall dries up, that is the effect you want. If the

environment is too humid for too long it becomes an incubation tank for bacteria which can cause lung infections and this is exacerbated by insect debris, skin shed, decaying leaves and so on. The problem is that no care sheet is written specifically with you and your chameleon in mind.

Yes, this book is a guideline designed to point you in the right direction but you need to observe how the water behaves in your cage. If it dries up after an hour, you need to mist more, if it's still wet after three hours, mist less. Unfortunately, its trial and error which is why it's always good for you to set up the environment and have a play around with humidity and moisture *before* bringing your chameleon home.

You Should Release Their Food And Leave It
The information on this is very contradictory. Yes, letting the feeder insects roam free in the cage is the best idea – it gives them exercise, provides them with activity and is as close to being in the wild as they're going to get. However, you still need to know how much they've eaten. Releasing ten crickets for example into the cage in the morning and noticing that there's none left in the afternoon so releasing more in isn't the best way to do it.

How do you know your chameleon hasn't just eaten two and the other eight aren't just hiding somewhere or worse, have escaped and are lurking about your house? The best way is to release the food but monitor how many your chameleon snaps up and try to remove any remaining afterwards. If you just leave the insects to run wild not only will they litter the cage but they may also turn on your lizard whilst they're asleep and start to bite them. (Not all insects will bite but some, like black crickets, will). I think it is good to place vegetables or fruit into the cage as well as the insects so they can continue to gut-load but also because they will most likely congregate around this food so will be easier to catch and remove.

117

Conclusion

Okay, so by now you should understand that Jackson's Chameleons aren't easy pets for the lazy owner. They are wild animals whose needs are often misunderstood.

If you love them and you are prepared to take care of them, well then by all means get one. They are wonderful, fascinating creatures. However, if you just want a novelty pet and you aren't interested in meeting their needs, preferring instead to just put them in a small cage where you can watch them for a while, then these aren't for you at all. I think rather than looking at them as just pets we should look at them as a hobby as well. They take up time and if you don't enjoy carrying out the tasks such as misting, checking temperatures, feeding and making adjustments, then this isn't for you.

The problem with Jackson's Chameleons is that their needs are often misunderstood. People think they are pretty, and whilst they are not the cheapest breed of chameleon they are in no way horrendously expensive. Some people purchase them thinking they will just sit in a cage in the corner of the room without realising how much work goes into them. They don't want to spend the money on lightbulbs and the other equipment needed nor do they want to spend hours researching the best way to look after them so they're placed next to a window with a bowl of water stagnating in the bottom of the cage and a few insects found in the garden are thrown in now and again. These chameleons then die and instead of the owner looking at themselves and saying "oh I didn't care for it properly" they say "oh Jackson's Chameleons are known for having a short life span".

The biggest killers of chameleons aren't glass enclosures and substrate – its owners. These aren't the easiest chameleon breed to look after and ideally months and months of careful research is needed and experimentation with temperature, humidity and heat is required BEFORE buying these creatures. Once bought they still need to be monitored and adjustments need to be made. These are living creatures yet their lives are cut short because we don't know how to care for them properly.

Another mistake people make is thinking that they're suitable for children. Yes, kids love them. Who wouldn't want a mini dinosaur in their bedroom? However, kids struggle to put a bowl of food down for a cat or often don't want to find the time to walk a dog once the novelty wears off. Kids are forgetful and impatient and loud. None of these qualities are great for a chameleon. What child wants to spend hours spraying water into a cage, feeding insects, adjusting temperature gauges and so on for an animal they can't even pick up and cuddle?

In short, I think Jackson's Chameleons are wonderful but I also think you need to be prepared for all the time and hard work that goes into them. Be prepared for the wiggly insects running about and making clicking sounds and other insect noises. Be prepared for said insects to escape and run about your house.

Be happy to build the perfect habitat and leave your Jackson's Chameleon to enjoy it in peace. In reality you are investing time and effort into a creature that won't give you a lot back personally – by this I mean you won't get love and cuddles and a pet that rushes to the front of its enclosure, wagging its tail because it's so excited to see you. At best you'll be treated with indifference, at worse you'll be treated in an aggressive manner. However, what you will get is an interesting pet and a feeling of contentment as your Jackson's Chameleon thrives and you can watch them bask and eat and go about their lives in a solitary, calm way.

www.ingramcontent.com/pod-product-compliance
Lightning Source LLC
Chambersburg PA
CBHW061959040426
42447CB00010B/1816